Embracing Technol in the Early Years

C000065698

Why should we embrace technology?
How can it make the practitioner's role easier?

This book is the answer to these questions, equipping Early Years practitioners with the skills and knowledge to use technology: both that which they already have, and that which they can access from beyond the setting (such as in the local community and online).

Written by an expert in both Early Years and Digital Inclusion, it provides practical tips and guidance for practitioners working at all levels to implement the use of technology across all areas of the curriculum and to support the development of the characteristics of effective learning. Drawing on contemporary theory and research, chapters cover key topics such as:

- the short and long-term benefits of incorporating technology for children, families, and staff

- making the most of pre-existing technology alongside guidance on how best to use new technology

- consideration of safeguarding issues around the use of technology with children

- technology beyond the setting and the use of local resources

- how technology can support professional development

- potential pitfalls of using technology

Containing links to curriculum and reflective prompts, this engaging and accessible book is essential reading for those interested in using technology to develop as a practitioner and continue to provide the best care and learning for every child.

Fiona Joines is an expert in early childhood education and digital technologies. This is her first book, and it draws on her passion for the Early Years and the wider world of technology.

Embracing Technology in the Early Years

A Practitioner's Guide

Fiona Joines

Routledge
Taylor & Francis Group

LONDON AND NEW YORK

Designed cover image: Fiona Joines

First edition published 2024
by Routledge
4 Park Square, Milton Park, Abingdon, Oxon, OX14 4RN

and by Routledge
605 Third Avenue, New York, NY 10158

Routledge is an imprint of the Taylor & Francis Group, an informa business

British Library Cataloguing-in-Publication Data
A catalogue record for this book is available from the British Library

Library of Congress Cataloging-in-Publication Data
Names: Joines, Fiona, 1977- author.
Title: Embracing technology in the early years : a practitioner's guide / Fiona Joines.
Description: Abingdon, Oxon ; New York, NY : Routledge, 2024. | Includes bibliographical references and index.
Identifiers: LCCN 2023012457 (print) | LCCN 2023012458 (ebook) | ISBN 9780367902094 (hardback) | ISBN 9780367902148 (paperback) | ISBN 9781003023173 (ebook)
Subjects: LCSH: Early childhood education--Computer-assisted instruction. | Educational technology. | Computers and children.
Classification: LCC LB1139.35.C64 J65 2024 (print) | LCC LB1139.35.C64 (ebook) | DDC 372.21--dc23/eng/20230426
LC record available at https://lccn.loc.gov/2023012457
LC ebook record available at https://lccn.loc.gov/2023012458

ISBN: 978-0-367-90209-4 (hbk)
ISBN: 978-0-367-90214-8 (pbk)
ISBN: 978-1-003-02317-3 (ebk)

DOI: 10.4324/9781003023173

Typeset in Bembo
by KnowledgeWorks Global Ltd.

Contents

Contents

Acknowledgements

This book was only possible thanks to the generous support and time of these brilliant humans: Kelly Atkinson; Bainton Road Nursery, Oxfordshire; Becky Bazeley; Emma Bromley; Emily Bunce; Charlton Acorns Pre-school, Oxfordshire; Mike Corlett; Susan Gibson; Grovelands Pre-school, Oxfordshire; Zoe Harvey; Karen Hunt; Sarah Jenkinson; Anita Joines; Ash Johnstone; Anoushka Karunanayake; Annamarie Kino; Becky Meadows; Cameron Shiell; and Christina Wakelin.

Introduction

This book is for all early years practitioners curious about using technology with the children and families you work with; whether you are dipping your toe in for the first time, revisiting it after a break, or are experienced in all things tech, I welcome you.

Use this book in the way that works for you and your colleagues. It is not a manual and does not attempt to cover every possible technological resource available, I have missed some out, some deliberately and some because I don't even know they exist yet (it's possible some of them didn't when I finished writing this book, but now do; things move fast).

Delve in, flick through, and return to it whenever you need a reminder, a refresher, or some inspiration.

I wrote the book to guide and support practitioners at any point in their journey of using technology with children but suggest it is especially useful for beginners and students (by which I mean anyone wanting to learn more).

It contains links to curriculum and ways of learning. It gives advice about resources, old tech, new tech, and the tech we encounter in everyday life. There are also suggestions about how to keep safe using technology and ways to avoid the pitfalls with examples of risk assessments to support your thinking.

You'll find links to using technology to support your own development and that of your colleagues and how to involve children and learn from them about technology.

By reading this book, I hope you will be more curious about technology, and be prepared to have a go, just as we encourage our children to do. I also hope you feel supported to find new ways to do things and test out your ideas.

DOI: 10.4324/9781003023173-1

Mostly, I hope this book helps you to develop as a practitioner and continue to provide the best care and learning for every child.

Reflective prompts

Before moving on to the next chapter, you might like to take a few moments and consider your own journey with technology. Here are some questions to help you do that.

- What technology did you have access to when you were growing up? What equipment was at home? What was available whilst you were in education?
- What technology do you use now and why? How does it benefit your life and that of your family?
- How does technology make you feel?
- What challenges do you face with technology and what skills do you have to help you overcome them?

Please note the following:

Parents is sometimes used alone but includes any adult with parental responsibility

Early Years Practitioner includes you if your role is about providing care and education for children up to age 8 although most references used relate to provision for under 5s.

1 Why Do I Need to Use Technology?

I am a technology enthusiast and I want you to be too, purely so you can make the best use of it for you, your families, and the children you care for. Children enjoy exploring all things new and exciting and can learn a lot from those experiences; having adults that embrace those experiences and resources alongside them can only enhance that.

I recognise that you may not be there yet, so this chapter explores the *why* of using technology in your work with children. The fact you've read this far suggests you want to explore what using technology means and that you are curious; what a brilliant mindset for working with children, thank you.

You might be nervous about technology for a range of reasons, many of which are understandable but, to give children what they need, nothing should be discounted without considering the benefits. What benefits will it bring to the children? How will it support the role of the practitioner? How will the team benefit? And what about the parents and families we work with? Of course, we also need to consider any drawbacks too.

In this chapter, this is exactly what we will explore. It will answer the questions of what the real benefits are and can be as well as consider the drawbacks and provide some reflective questions to help you do the same.

Theory as a starting point

As anyone who has ever been in one of my training sessions knows, I love theory and I take every opportunity to get it into relevant areas of any topic. It underpins our practice and helps us to find a way through when there are other things often getting in the way of what we know is right. It helps me to

DOI: 10.4324/9781003023173-2

argue my case with anyone I need to about why certain practices are "right" over others and gets people to rethink the way they do things or explain what might be going on. Theory is important to me and so it feels right I start this book from a place of theory. Some of the sections have been influenced by Goldschmied's work on the Key Person approach, or Piaget's ideas around thought processes and making links. Some by Bandura's social learning theory and a focus on positive reinforcement, or Montessori's following the child. Although not necessarily explicitly cited in the book, I'm sure you'll spot the links.

For the purpose of this book and the subject of technology in early years, we will focus on theory that links to social learning and that of technology for learning. I have also picked out a few key pieces of research to support the use of technology with children.

This chapter will consider Vygotsky and his work around social learning, the importance of a more experienced other, and the zone of proximal development (ZPD). We will then look at scaffolding with links to Bruner and the spiral curriculum popularised by Moyles (Pound 2009) as well as theory around a child-centred approach.

Next, I will explore the ideas of digital natives and the importance of a hands-on approach to learning, especially with technology. There are links to research by Ofcom, NAYEC, and the office of the Children's Commissioner and others. You will find all the links at the end of the chapter so you can read them in full and I urge you to do this.

Social learning theory

We are social creatures and as such many of us thrive when we have connection with others. We also learn from and with others so social learning theory developed by Albert Bandura (Pound 2005) makes a lot of sense. The theory focuses on how we learn by watching and imitating those around us and as such the importance of role models became clear. Children (and adults) will copy the behaviour of those around them to "fit in" and to belong, but there are also internal processes that help the child (and adult) decide which behaviours to copy; it is not automatic. We develop our understanding of what is right and wrong and so can make a choice about when we copy or not. We see this in action when young children look towards an adult before they join in with a game they wonder if really they should be playing such as "jumping on a sofa" or "kicking sand in the sandpit." Some children developing their inner conscious will want to join in but stop and consider if it is right. The look to the adult shows they want confirmation it is ok.

Children learn lots of things by watching, mimicking, and joining in with others. They learn personal skills such as getting dressed or washing, how to care for books, and how to play with others. They also learn how to use equipment such as technological toys by watching others and having a go.

Zone of proximal development

The theory of the ZPD developed by Vygotsky (Pound 2005) and illustrated in Figure 1.1 is one of my favourites and I see links to this in so many areas of my work. So, what is it? In a nutshell, it is "what a child can do with support of a more experienced or skilled other." So, when a child is supported by an adult or crucially a peer, they move from what they can do to what might be possible. They stretch and challenge their abilities and test out ways of doing things with the support of that other person. It is enabling a child to move from their comfort zone, zone of actual development, into their ZPD or the "what next" area.

This theory is sprinkled all the way through the EYFS where it talks about the skills required by the practitioners to observe, assess, and plan for the children in their care, through the theme of positive relationships and throughout the characteristics of effective learning.

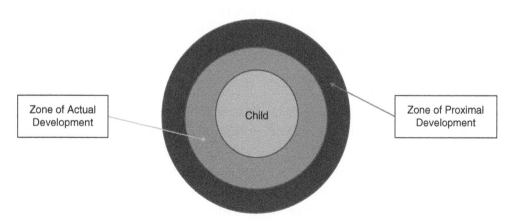

Figure 1.1 A chart to illustrate the zone of proximal development (ZPD). Chart created by F Joines.

Scaffolding

Jerome Bruner (Pound 2005) has influenced current practice in lots of ways; the term scaffolding was coined by him and the idea built on Vygotsky's work on ZPD. Scaffolding is where the adult assists the child with their learning by adding a "scaffold" to support the process. Parents do this with young children, for example, when they are first using words and practitioners do it for a whole range of learning from putting on coats, to reading, to baking, and woodwork. As the child develops the skill, the adult gradually removes the scaffolding so the child can be independent in that skill.

Bruner also introduced us to the spiral curriculum, that is where a child revisits learning experiences to develop the skills and knowledge around it. We know as early years practitioners that repetition is important for learning. Children often return to things deemed too easy for them to repeat the learning to consolidate it or to build on it by making links to more complex learning. Janet Moyles did much to build on this work and when describing her play spiral talked about ripples being created outwards from free play with the support of an adult through "playful teaching." (How children learn 3 – contemporary thinking and theorists, 2009.)

The child at the centre

Putting the child at the centre of what we do seems entirely logical. It feels instinctive to include those who we are working with in their learning and play. It is, in my view, best practice to ensure children have agency and some control over their play and learning as they often know what they need. They revisit learning as mentioned above in relation to the spiral curriculum, they play alongside others, social learning, and they reach out to others for "scaffolding" and "teaching" from more experienced others. Of course, skilled practitioners are key to creating the enabling environment required for these to take place and guide the child along their journey to continue to develop but the child must be a part of that. The positive relationship is key.

As well as his work on the ZPD, Vygotsky (Pound 2005) believed that children absorb what is around them. So, clear links to the enabling environment, role models, and social learning. Lave and Wegner (1991) focused a lot of their work on communities of practice which talks about shared experiences and working together to problem solve which we observe often within our settings. However, they also recognise the importance of the support from others (practitioners), just being in the space is not enough.

Theory and technology

Children learn about a range of things in this way and technology is certainly one. They see it being used by others everywhere, at home with adults using microwaves, washing machines, TVs, and mobile phones. They see it in the community when pressing the button for the green man at road crossings, using self-service checkouts or checking into the GP surgery. They see it at nursery, when they arrive and press the intercom, when staff capture their play on cameras or when they use tablets to record observations.

The theories outlined fit within social constructivism but in 2005 Siemens made the point that we should reconsider the learning theories as technology was "rewiring the brain" and therefore the way we learn is changing. He used the term "connectivism" which focuses on learning by making links and drew on Chaos theory (the theory that everything is connected to everything) to support his thinking. This connects to the characteristics of effective learning and our approach to early years clearly alongside the spiral curriculum and repetitive nature of how children learn.

"On the Horizon" published a paper in 2001 by Marc Prensky that introduced the idea of digital immigrants and digital natives: the theory talked about how those who were born before the mid-1990s had not grown up "with" and "surrounded" by technology. They had come to it as immigrants, learning about it later on in their learning journey, whereas those born from mid-1990s were "digital natives" born surrounded by the digital age. In the paper, he makes the statement that the education system was no longer fit for the children of today (2001), mostly due to the digital age.

Ten years later, in 2011, the digital immigrants and digital natives' idea was developed by David White as the idea of people being in a distinct camp did not quite work with real people. The continuum of "Visitors and Residents" proposes the idea that each of us is somewhere along the line of being "users or members" of the web, either using the web as a tool or a place as any other for socialising and so on. This continuum is fluid and we can move our position as required. This reflects the real world more accurately as each person's experiences and background will impact their access to and the availability of the digital world. This, therefore, feels more relevant to the world of early years. Some of the children we work with will be growing up surrounded by the digital world, others will have glimpses, and some will have no access at all. It also means the workforce, us, will each sit somewhere along this continuum. Some colleagues will have grown up submerged within the digital world and some of us will have come to it later, regardless of when we were born. I was born in 1977 so I'm certainly not a digital native but have had opportunities through work and home to develop a love for using technology for lots of things in all areas of my life. On the continuum, I would put myself very firmly at the resident's end.

Where are you and what impact does that have on your views around technology?

What about the children you work with? I've heard the current generation being referred to as "YouTube Kids" to literally mean those growing up with YouTube and 89% of children aged 3–17 are accessing it regularly (Ofcom, 2022). What impact might this have on their development? On their perspective on technology? On how they see the world?

What does it mean to us?

The theory helps us to explore and explain what might be going on, but it also shows up some challenges that we will have to face and overcome.

It shows us that even if we have not grown-up with technology, we are able to adapt to it, use it, and even become a member of the digital world. So, we all have the capacity to make effective use of technology, but we may simply not want to or feel able to. We will know of practitioners that struggle to see the value of using technology in the early years, those who simply opt out, and those that are not confident with using it. We'll also know of colleagues that are intimidated by technology for a range of reasons. None of this is insurmountable providing the practitioner has a "have a go" attitude, is prepared to try something with an open mind and see what happens. If practitioners close off their minds to the use of technology, or any other aspect of the world, they risk what they provide being ineffective. Learning and teaching is most effective when provided and guided by open-minded and open-hearted practitioners.

Lesley Abbott and Tina Bruce (Pound 2009), among others, are strong advocates of children being able to have a go and enjoy real hands-on experiences to aid their learning. I think there are very few early years practitioners who would disagree with that approach and it is true for whatever children are learning, so technology is included. They need to see, touch, hear, (smell and taste!) the objects, explore them, discover for themselves what they can do, try new ways of using it, solve problems in new ways ... you'll recognise these as characteristics of effective learning. They make sense.

Current research

Many organisations carry out research in the field of early years and technology and I have drawn on a few key pieces to support this book that you may find useful and interesting as you do your own research in the area.

Each year, Ofcom researches the media attitudes of children and parents. The papers show how things are shifting in this world, in terms of access and attitudes of using technology and allowing it into our homes. It tells us what children are doing whilst online and which social media platforms they have accounts on, even when they are under the age to have a profile. This research helps us to understand childrens' and parents' concerns about the digital world and how well equipped both groups feel able to stay safe or keep their children safe online.

For the youngest children in the survey, it is their parents who are questioned but older children speak for themselves, and it provides some reassuring news that most do know about safety measures and ways to report issues online (https://www.ofcom.org.uk/__data/assets/pdf_file/0024/234609/childrens-media-use-and-attitudes-report-2022.pdf).

The EU Kids Online project gathers data about what children aged 9–16 are doing online from across Europe (there are also parallel projects happening in other parts of the world). This is useful, as it shows us what is to come for our young children. It can also help to shape and inform policy that will affect all children such as the setting of age limits for social media platforms, identifying the risks and how to reduce them, and attempting to reduce barriers to access for children from more disadvantaged backgrounds. This link explains the project and the full report from 2020 is available along with a short introductory video if you want to know more (https://www.lse.ac.uk/media-and-communications/research/research-projects/eu-kids-online).

You can read more about the digital divide amongst families in this report from the Sutton Trust. The report also talks about how three organisations responded to lockdown to continue supporting families through technology (https://www.suttontrust.com/news-opinion/all-news-opinion/the-digital-divide-includes-families-in-the-early-years/).

In 2018, the Department for Education carried out research and did a follow-up survey in 2020 with families with children aged 0–5 years which included sections about using apps and home-learning. You can read more here: https://www.gov.uk/government/publications/childcare-and-early-years-survey-of-parents-2018-follow-up-survey-report and here: https://assets.publishing.service.gov.uk/government/uploads/system/uploads/attachment_data/

file/866868/Childcare_and_early_years_survey_of_parents_2018_follow-up_survey.pdf

Next, we will consider the benefits and drawbacks to using technology.

Benefits to child

When providing environments and resources in a play setting, the priority must be "what's in it for the child?" What will they get out of the experience? What are the possibilities? As effective practitioners, we will be basing our responses to these based on sound knowledge of child development, good awareness of the EYFS, and our understanding of where the child is and where they are going next.

Invariably, children will take what you have provided and do something even more wondrous and purposeful. They will create their own way and will teach us something we had not even considered. Surely, that is one of the many and varied reasons we do what we do.

We consider these aspects and provide a wide range of resources, a safe space, and highly skilled adults. So, why should we include technology as part of this? It is often closed in its use and offers one way of doing something, requires an electrical source or batteries, and there may only be one. But there are real benefits of using technology within the setting and I am going to set out some of those below.

Gaining skills

When I was a child, I was rarely allowed to "control" the TV or radio. They were adult things and adults controlled them. Although, because there was no TV remote, sometimes the adult would ask me (or a sibling) to switch over the channel or alter the volume so the adult did not have to get up. What a treat!

Seriously, technology was not for children … and here I am, an adult, having to use technology (for everything). I have had to learn how to use it as an adult, when learning is harder to do, our children have a chance to learn about it when learning is the most natural thing in the world for them. So, let us make the most of this opportunity.

Ready for the future

Technology has always been a part of our lives and will continue to be. The technology has developed and become more advanced and more complicated than we could have imagined, and it continues to develop. By using a range of technology-based toys, children are acquiring the skills that will enable them to live in the real world as they grow and become adults. It will give them the ability to engage with whatever the world of technology has to come in ways that those from earlier generations did not have. Some of us have had the challenging task of adapting to everyday technology that is completely new to us. Let us give the children an advantage by allowing their exploration of this equipment now.

Foundations

Our role is about ensuring children can reach their full potential and this is not just whilst they are in our care, but lifelong. Early years lay the foundations for life; a love of learning, underpinning skills, and how to form relationships. The things children develop with us lead them to live full and valuable lives. This includes being able to embrace change, try new things, and continue to be curious about the world around them. Technology is a great tool for all of this and more. Much of the technology children will have access to once they begin work will not even exist yet and will require people to show curiosity, be determined and resilient, find solutions, and make things work. We cannot afford to have children grow up into adults who are fearful or ignorant of technology the way that many previous generations have been.

Play

There is no getting away from the fact that lots of technology can provide hours and hours of fun. I imagine that many of you reading this will spend time playing with one technology or another. Time on Facebook, playing cards, taking photographs, baking with a whizzy food mixer … it has become a usual pastime. And surely if we can play with technology, we want children to as well?

I love a new "toy." I love playing with the equipment, seeing what this bit will do, what happens when I press this. I played for hours when I got my new mobile, my new laptop, my Bluetooth speaker, my food mixer, my sewing machine … I just could not help but try them out, and I smiled a lot whilst doing it. I also got frustrated, a bit cross, sad that it would not do what I thought it would and felt sheer delight when I managed to do things I had not done before. In short, technology is fun. Well, it can be. Certainly, for children who approach all of their experiences with play. They see the fun in all of the technology resources, the walkie-talkies, the metal detectors, the music players, and so on. There is nothing wrong with that … so enable the fun to happen, let them play.

Children play differently to us; they are freer and more open to possibilities than adults often are. They do not consider the rules of play in the way we do and are happy to use objects in more creative ways. They might take things apart, use them to represent other objects, simply "pretend" to use them or find something we had not even thought of to do with the item. You will see the concentration on their faces as they work out how something works and the joy as they discover a new use. They may stay focused on one item for a moment, for many minutes, or the whole session, returning to it over and over again to try something new. But they will have fun.

Children use any item they can find to support their problem solving, they also use each other. So, once again as the adult, we can encourage this by providing a wide range of equipment and tools. We can pose problems and create invitations to play that provoke questions from the children and engage them in finding solutions. We can teach them how to use an internet search engine to find answers to questions in the way we would have had an adult get out encyclopaedia Britannica …

Child-led play

Children are naturally curious and inquisitive, so we need to encourage that, but it needs to be in a child-led way. They need to be given choice and adults need to allow them to have control over their play. This supports the development of other skills and prioritises the characteristics of effective learning which are discussed later in this book.

We talk about child-led learning when we describe pedagogy in early years, following the child's interests, letting them have autonomy over their play and being in control of it. Enabling children to use resources, space, and their imaginations openly and with freedom. Using technological resources is a part of that pedagogy. If a child is using a technology resource, they are in control, they turn it on and off, press the buttons, make it move, create sounds and lights, and determine what they can do with it. Almost all technology resource can be child-led, that is to say, operated by the child.

Transference of learning

Also, if children develop more independence in one area, they are likely to transfer that to other areas so as they become used to their independence and freedom.

In my experience, children are really good at knowing what they need to develop at what time. They focus on what they need to consolidate or to practice and they know when they need to challenge and push themselves.

Children often enjoy the freedom to try things for themselves and to develop those skills they see as important at that moment. Rather than an adult planning for that skill, children can do this in their own time. They will also find a way to develop what they need that may not be how, as an adult, we might have guided them. That is learning, and it shows a real "can do attitude."

Supporting social interactions

Above I have talked about how children can control their own play and be independent, but technology can and does also enable interaction with others, in lots of ways. Some of the resources such as walkie-talkies only work with two people – no good talking to yourself (well, sometimes it *is* helpful). Some resources can be used alone but provide even more fun when used with others such as a music player – dancing and singing with others is always more uplifting. Some resources provide lovely opportunities to develop turn taking such as a camera or a voice recorder.

The other way technology can support and develop interaction is of course whilst online – having a video call where you can see the people at the other end – sharing news, stories, ideas, and feelings whilst not being in the same room. Making connections with people that we may never get to meet in real life – lots of settings have set up twinning projects where they share their experiences with settings in other parts of the country or world. It is a lovely way for the children to interact and learn about other ways of living. There are clear links to cultural capital here too.

Benefits to staff

Of course, the child is the most important: we put them at the centre of our practice and our pedagogy starts and ends with them but there are benefits to staff in using technology in your work too.

If children can be autonomous in their play, in control of their play, we can focus on supporting them in different ways. We can observe them in more meaningful ways and step back from their play. We can provide support from the sidelines, offering encouragement, extensions, and this helps us resist the urge to interfere with their play. We can observe the environment more, noticing the space and how children use it. We can then of course respond to our observations and adapt and change based on real live feedback from our children.

Technology can then be utilised here to help us with those tasks.

Observation

Observing children is a key aspect of working with them and the skill is one we get better at with time and practice, and technology can support this process. When we first meet a child, we are already observing, assessing, and wondering how they might come into our setting (even if we do not recognise that we are). We notice things about the child that will help us support their transition into the setting and ask questions of the child and their parent to confirm our observations. If you have not noticed yourself doing this, observe a colleague next time a child and their parent are in your setting on a show-round; you will see it in others. I do not recommend using technology to do this early-stage observation.

Once a child starts with us officially, our observations become more "formal" in that we note things, we write long observations and use a variety of ways, and track progress.

You might choose to record your observations using technology such as taking photographs, capturing a voice recording, filming the space, or typing on to a tablet. With some of the software available, you can then add this directly to a child's file and the software can help you analyse the observation, which can be a real time saver. Storage of those observations is secure as standard and sharing is simple too.

A note about observations

The skill of observation should not be underestimated and for anyone new to that skill, you can practise and get better at it. I understand that the process of observing children can feel hard, that you cannot write quickly enough to capture "everything," and your writing becomes illegible. Be patient, practise, and it will become easier. You will also start to notice things and capturing them when not formally observing and then your observations will be more meaningful and enable you to use them more usefully. As a student, you might have been asked to create situations to observe children doing certain types of activities so you could meet specific criteria in a module for example. That is not how it works, not quite. If your setting creates an enabling environment, knows the children well, and places them at the heart of what they do, children will engage in a range of resources and activities, meaning the practitioner can observe them in all areas of the curriculum and not have to "create" situations just to observe.

Observation is something we are doing all the time and we are always responding to these observations to ensure the child is getting what they need at the right time.

So, observation is the key to finding where a child is, to find out their interests, their abilities, their skills, what they know, what they do not know, what they dislike, and so on. Observation is a skill that we can learn and practice to improve, and observation does not have to be formal to be effective. What is your next step to develop your own observation skills?

Sharing information with families

If we can communicate with parents in a way that suits them we are more likely to have a positive relationship with them, so being able to share observations as you record them in a shared space is really helpful. Parents are able to access them at a time that suits them and can make comments and respond to those observations. This is obviously a benefit to parents too.

Space

Another way technology can support the staff's role is by helping us assess and audit our spaces. It is easy to leave everything as it is for too long without stepping back and considering the impact the environment has on all of us. Regularly reviewing and moving the space around will support the children's learning; technology can be used here in really simple ways. For example, taking photographs of the space at different times of the day will help you to see how the children use the space. This allows the team to analyse that and make changes, even a small one can make a big difference, but it can be hard to see what needs changing whist you are "in" the space. By keeping those images, you have a clear record of when the space was laid out in that way and can then make note of when to repeat the process to check everything is still working.

You could also take photographs from different perspectives such as down low (where the children are) to see how it looks and feels.

Reflecting on practice

Technology is useful when we are reflecting on our practice in a few ways. One is that we might choose to record our reflections in a digital format such as an online journal, or sound, or video recordings. We might use an online tool to capture key thoughts such as Jamboard or Mural.

We might also use the internet to research and discover new ways of reflecting or sharing our practice with others in online forums, social media groups, or by setting up video calls with one or more colleagues to talk about a specific topic of practice.

Training

There is a plethora of training opportunities online. You can find e-learning and webinars on almost any topic, some which are self-directed, some where you learn "live" with a facilitator and other learners. Many conferences are held digitally now so you can log in to sessions that might otherwise have been inaccessible due to location, cost, or the time of day/week they are held.

You can access training by watching TED talks or documentaries and there is a wealth of reading.

A word of caution though for all of the online materials, before you commit your time and money (or your organisations'), check who is providing it and what their incentive is to do so. Are they a reputable organisation with the sector? Are they supported by governmental bodies, a corporate organisation, or charities? Do they ground the work in research and peer review? Has someone recommended them to you?

Children's independence in play

Technology supports children to play alongside others and supports their sharing and turn taking skills. It also leads to children modelling for each other – how to use equipment, how to make it work, how to care for it, what words to use, creative ways of using it, and so on. How does this benefit us? If children are learning to be more collegiate in their play, they need us a little less. When they learn from each other, they need us a little less.

Communication

One big advantage of technology for us as practitioners is allowing us to make communication with families even easier. It provides a whole array of alternative ways to keep in touch with families and engage them in the work we do to teach and care for their children. We all have families that are harder to reach for a range of reasons so having a bigger variety of ways to connect with them will surely help. Some families find it hard to spend time in the setting during drop off and collection times

Benefits to families

Communication works best when it is two-way, so practitioners sharing information with families will benefit them too as they can share information with us easier and in a way that suits them best. It makes us, the practitioner, more accessible and helps to develop the partnership working in new ways.

Being able to share something personal that might impact the child may feel too real if shared within the setting but sending a message can help as it adds a distance. Sharing the child's first steps via your online learning journal while it happens is special and could not be recreated the next day in the session. Sending a text to explain a late arrival might be the only way a parent can fit in letting you know, whilst they are mopping the kitchen floor after the burst pipe and in between getting the children dressed and fed ready for their day.

Families want the best for their children now and for their futures, so using technology and exposing children to its uses is preparing them for the future. The children will be gaining and developing skills that will be useful throughout their lives, and, as we have already acknowledged, technology is not going away.

Lots of parents may have limited skills in using technology or low confidence to use anything "new" so by us using technology to communicate and share information we help them to develop their skills too, and this in turn will help them to support their children with technology use.

Of course, it is fair to say that we struggle to engage some parents no matter what mediums of communication we try, but if we use a wider variety, we have a much higher chance of something working for each family.

As experts on child development, the EYFS, observation techniques, and all other aspects of working with children you know that we always put the child at the heart of what we do. This starts when we first meet the child and continues throughout their time in our care.

School readiness and reaching potential

School readiness has been on the agenda for a long time as it is a key function of the Early Years Foundation Stage (EYFS). *It promotes teaching and learning to ensure children's 'school readiness' and gives children the broad range of knowledge and skills that provide the right foundation for good future progress through school and life.* (EYFS 2017) We know that the early years are the prime time for children to develop the full range of underpinning skills to set them up for a fulfilling future and the EYFS has a major part to play in that.

School readiness is about children being ready for the next phase in life, in all ways. In recent years, there has been some debate about what this looks like. For some, it is seen as children being able to follow instructions (do as they are told), sit on the carpet without fidgeting, and write their name. These are adult-focused tasks and many of those working in the sector do not see these things as the most important. Instead, they list such things as curiosity, social skills, and having some independence over their personal care (PACEY, 2013). These link directly to both the characteristics of effective learning and to the prime area of personal, social, and emotional development.

Technological resources, many of which I share later, provide opportunities to be curious and to develop their love of learning in ways that differ from the more traditional. I also discuss that children love to share with their peers how to use "new" equipment which promotes a range of social skills. Finally, using a range of technology in the early years exposes them to how the world works, and how we interact with the world, further supporting them to transition to school.

Reflective prompts – Why do I need to use technology?

Having read about some of the theory and research that support the use of technology within the sector, take a few minutes to reflect on this chapter.

- Consider your own approach to working with children, which theories influence that approach? Also consider the approach of the setting.

- How do you see technology fitting into that approach?

- Why do you use technology in your setting? Does this fit with the approach you use? Consider your use in relation to working with the children, their families, and as a staff team.

Conclusion

This chapter has set out why I believe technology should be embraced in the sector.

It started by looking to a range of theories, including very current theory to ensure there is good pedagogical reasoning behind what I set out, and supporting the stage we are each at in our own journey with technology.

I have also set out a wide range of benefits to using technology in the sector, benefits for us, benefits for the families and most importantly, benefits for the children we work with.

Where to read more about the theories and research discussed in this chapter

You can read more about some of the theories and research mentioned in this chapter at the following links/book recommendations.

The "How Children Learn" suite of books by Linda Pound are some of the best and most accessible in my opinion.

The original "How Children Learn" includes profiles on theorists such as Vygotsky, Bruner, and Bandura.

The 3rd book "How Children Learn 3 – Contemporary thinking and theorists" (2009) includes Abbott, Bruce, and Moyles.

They are all published by Practical Pre-School Books and available directly from the publishers website https://practicalpreschoolbooks.com/

Planning Play and the Early Years by Penny Tassoni and Karen Hucker, first published in 2000 by Heinemann Educational Publishers, is for me still one of the best books to remind me of some fundamentals about play; I dip into it regularly.

In addition to the books above, I used a range of research papers which are listed below with a link to them online (which was correct at time of writing).

Communities of Practice – Lave, J, & Wenger, E (1991). Situated learning: Legitimate peripheral participation. https://infed.org/mobi/jean-lave-etienne-wenger-and-communities-of-practice/

Technology and Social Constructivism – George Siemans (2005). http://itdl.org/Journal/Jan_05/article01.htm

On the Horizon Immigrants and Natives – Prensky (2001). https://www.marcprensky.com/writing/Prensky%20-%20Digital%20Natives,%20Digital%20Immigrants%20-%20Part1.pdf

Visitor and Residents – David White, DS & Le Cornu, A (2011). Visitors and Residents: A new typology for online engagement. *First Monday*, 16, (9). https://ualresearchonline.arts.ac.uk/id/eprint/8528/

2 How Can Technology Support the Characteristics of Effective Learning and Areas of Learning?

The Early Years statutory framework (March 2021) that came into effect from 1st September 2021 sets out the requirements for three areas: 1) Learning and Development, 2) Assessment, and 3) Safeguarding and Welfare. We need to be clear that this framework is not a curriculum to tell practitioners how to meet these requirements, it is setting out the minimum standards every child should have access to when they attend one of the various types of early years settings available in England including those who attend childminders' settings.

Since the 2012 version of the Early Years Foundation Stage, the characteristics of effective learning have been central to our approach within the sector. Alongside these, we have the areas of learning. In this chapter, I talk about both of these and make links to them and to technology but I start with the CofEL.

The most effective tools for developing CofEL are open-ended materials that do not have a clear outcome. So, "how can technology fit in?" is what this chapter will cover.

The CofEL

CofEL are the ways we learn. They are the strategies we develop to enable us to access and explore the world around us, the range of approaches that, once established, can be used and adapted across all aspects of our lives as we grow right throughout adulthood. They are fundamental to us being successful citizens and functioning adults. If we have a set of well-established characteristics of effective learning, we can learn anything, do anything, and therefore, be anything.

DOI: 10.4324/9781003023173-3

Practitioners need to provide all children with opportunities to explore at a pace that suits them and in a way that is accessible and therefore recognises the unique child. If children develop an intrinsic motivation to learn, to explore and investigate, to try their own ideas, and to simply have a go, they can tackle anything that life might throw at them. Their love of learning will remain always.

Playing and exploring

Children try things out, investigate the world around them, and are prepared to "have a go" at opportunities that are provided for them or that they create for themselves. This is about encouraging children to use what is around them to discover things about themselves, each other, and the world they are growing up in. The role of the adult therefore is to ensure we provide a rich, diverse, and sensory environment for them to engage in that discovery learning. Technology has to form a part of that environment if children are to be given that variety and to learn about the wider world.

Active learning

Children spend focused time on their play and try different ways to overcome difficulties they may experience. Children show intrinsic motivation to try things out, to stay focused for increasingly long periods of time, and to "keep on trying" when something doesn't go as planned. We see children celebrating success when something works or they achieve "what they set out to do." Technology fits well here as some online programmes and technology tools give feedback to encourage the player or user to try again such as the games on the CBeebies website, which give encouragement with verbal cues, music, and images.

Creating and thinking critically

Children come up with their own ideas and are able to make links between what they know and what they are learning. Children create new ways to do things and try them out, experimenting with all that they know and making decisions as they go. They plan out and predict what might happen, and practice reviewing what worked and what didn't. Again, we can see technology has a place to support this characteristic; for example, if a child selects a camera to play with, they will capture images of the world from a very different perspective to an adult, they will also experiment with angles, viewpoints, and notice things adults often miss.

Technology can also support problem-solving skills; for example, whilst playing in the sandpit, a child loses a badge they were wearing. The badge is made of metal. One way of finding it might be a metal detector. Or, a child has a question no one knows the answer to, so how can we solve this problem together? A search engine on the web will likely help us to solve this.

The EYFS

"The EYFS is based around 7 areas of learning and in the 2012 revision of the EYFS placed a stronger emphasis on the *ways* children learn, in order to support practitioners with understanding their role within a play-based curriculum (Tickell, 2011), this helped to shift the focus away from *what* children learn." The latest version of the statutory framework, 2021 attempts to move the emphasis further towards the "how" of children's learning and that is a welcome development. The latest revision has seen changes that have implications for settings such as the explicit addition of the requirement to focus on oral health and implications for this book as the early learning goal focusing on technology has been removed. Until the 2021 EYFS, practitioners were supporting children to "recognise that a range of technology is used in places such as homes and schools. They select and use technology for particular purposes" (Department for Education, 2017). The removal of this early learning goal does not mean that we no longer provide opportunities for children to play and explore using technology, or to learn about technology, it just means it isn't formally measured.

We still have a responsibility to teach children about technology and to teach them about the world by using technology. It is a part of the life skills that will take them through childhood into adulthood.

There are non-statutory guidance documents that are designed to support us. The practitioner, with further explanation of the CofEL and suggestions for ways practitioners can support these in their practice. Being non-statutory you can choose which, if any, you use and of course you can use a combination to find the best fit for you, the setting and most of all the children. These include Development Matters and Birth to 5 Matters. That freedom to do what is right for the children and families accessing your setting is crucial to meeting their needs.

Areas of learning

The EYFS provides us with clear guidance on the areas of learning and breaks these into two key areas, the prime areas and the specific areas.

The prime areas are those which underpin a child's learning and should be the focus of our work with children under two years of age, and then should continue right through the early years. They are Personal, Social, and Emotional development, Physical development, and Communication and Language. They are fundamental to our development and link directly to how our brain is developing from birth to three years old.

The specific areas build on the prime areas and should only be focused on once the prime areas are established. The specific areas are Mathematical development, Literacy, Understanding the World, and Expressive Arts and Design.

So, how can we still use technology in our practice whilst meeting the requirements set out for us?

As I mention throughout the book, technology is all around us and hard to ignore. It has become even more present in our lives since the recent global pandemic. Children are exposed to technology in the home, and out in the community. It seems right then that we should provide them with the tools, skills, and knowledge about how to use technology to enhance their worlds.

Communication and language

The focus here is spoken language, what children hear and say within the language rich environment you create within your setting. It's about sharing stories, singing together, and exploring sounds, rhythms, and rhymes. It's nurturing a love of language, playing with words, and role playing characters. Technology can be a part of this exploration and play; for example, a simple "talking peg" or "button" can be used by children to record their voices over and over or an app on a tablet can do the same thing but has a longer memory so children can tell stories and listen back to them too.

Physical development

Moving our bodies and being active is important for development as well as physical and mental health and this area of learning is all about how and why we move; practicing skills and noticing how our bodies move, what happens when we move quickly, when we move softly, and when we are still. Getting stronger, developing coordination, and gaining control of our body are all part of this area. Using technology here is about developing our fine motor skills to control the devices and equipment as well as using it to track what our bodies do such as a stopwatch to see how much time passes when we do an activity such as hop on one leg.

Personal, social, and emotional development

What are we without others? This area of learning helps us find out about ourselves and those around us whilst supporting us to build relationships with those people in a safe and loving way. This also develops our sense of self, identify and process our emotions, and learn how to self-regulate our feelings. We learn by watching those around us and so the key person along with the wider staff team (when there is one) is crucial in modelling what a healthy relationship is, boundary setting and managing our emotions. Seeing ourselves on a screen, looking at our face as we express ourselves, helps us recognise what that feeling is and to talk about it. Watching programmes designed for children about feelings helps us to process that too and any equipment that requires turn taking supports our social learning. Teaching peers how to use equipment such as a camera or metal detector in the garden, rather than relying on only adults being the "teacher," is great for a child's PSE development too.

Literacy

This area of learning focuses on reading and writing, and encourages children to develop a love of them, in particular reading. We have to understand the words we use as well as recognise them on the page (or screen) and once again the adult's role is crucial and directly links to communication and language. It requires children to see written words in context so they start to make links and it requires adults reading with them. How can technology support this? Mark-making ultimately leads to writing, but we can create marks with tech too such as touchscreen devices which can be more intuitive than a pencil.

Mathematics

Developing a sense of what numbers are is important as all other maths builds on this. Supporting children to notice patterns and make connections with the world around them is a part of this. The vocabulary around numbers is also important so our role as adults is clear again, and seeing shapes, recognising spaces, and measuring area are all key elements here. There are lots of technology tools that we can employ here such as calculators and timers, cameras and computers. A light box has a number of uses here when exploring shapes too.

Understanding the world

Making sense of the world around us; the things we see, hear, taste, smell, and touch are all part of this area of learning. Every experience a child has helps to shape this understanding, every interaction and every visit adds to their learning. So, the richer and more varied those experiences, visits, and interactions are the more equipped a child is to understand and therefore be a part of the world. Technology can help offer some of these experiences we wouldn't otherwise be able to access such as using video calls to meet and talk with people from other parts of the world, other communities, and other walks of life. Using a metal detector in the garden to find out what is under the earth together or a telescope to see the stars all develop our sense of the world around us.

Expressive arts and design

Children have endless imagination if the adults around them nurture it and a wild imagination can lead to all sorts of creative endeavours as well as being able to find wonder and beauty everywhere. This area is another one that calls on all of our senses so as adults we need to ensure we provide a multi-sensory environment with opportunities to explore a wide range of materials. Children should be encouraged to express themselves freely and in a variety of ways that reflect that personal expression. They also need to be encouraged to be curious and open to new ways of doing things and the ways others may choose to express themselves too. Technology tools that can be used include cameras for capturing the world from their view, smart speakers and music players for exploring a wider range of music and sounds and moving to them or a karaoke machine to sing along to.

Ages and stages

Each child will grow and develop in their own time with the right environment and adults around them to support and facilitate this; however, in general terms there are stages and phases of development that we expect children to progress through.

To support our understanding of the non-statutory guidance, Development Matters talks about the following stages: Birth to 3, 3- and 4-year-olds, and children in reception to provide guidance on what children will be learning in this stage and examples of how we can provide opportunities for this development to progress.

The Birth to 5 Matters document uses narrower ranges of age which overlap to guide practitioners. The ranges are: 0–6 months, 6–12 months, 12–18 months, 18–24 months, 24–36 months, 36–48 months, 48–60 months, and 60–71 months. The overlapping is especially important to remind us that children and their development are not linear and are unique to the child.

However, having some general guidance can help us and so, with that in mind, the next section of the chapter gives some examples directly relating to using technology.

0–12 months

For our very youngest children, anything that beeps, spins, or flashes such as spinning tops, push button toys, and night lights in the sleep room could be considered technology and age appropriate. Babies have very short attention spans and therefore any worries of children spending too long with these items should be set aside. The World Health Organisation (WHO) recommends no sedentary screen time for those under 1 and that when a child is sedentary, a caregiver shares stories or similar with them. So, as a professional early years practitioner, it would be advisable to follow these guidelines recognising that parents may make other decisions.

Windup toys, mobiles, light cubes, activity mats (or something similar wall mounted), pull-back vehicles, pop-up toys, musical books, and soft toys that talk when squeezed are all examples of equipment that are appropriate for under 1s and provides them with exposure to the world of technology without harm, although you should still assess the risk of the equipment regularly; see Chapter 3 for more information on risk assessments. A key point to make here is that this age group requires a caring adult to play closely alongside them, to demonstrate the equipment, and to create a safe and enabling environment.

By introducing such toys, we can support the young child's curiosity in the world, their sense of awe and wonder and they will start to develop their hand-eye coordination by using the equipment and making it work.

12–36 months

As children grow and become more mobile, they need opportunities for more independent exploration in their environment and adults can start to supervise beyond arm's length. All of the toys they've had access to whilst babies are still of interest and provide consolidation of learning as well as allowing children to use them in new ways. You might also start to introduce a wider range of those and toys that support physical development such as activity walkers or toy vacuum cleaners. This type of toy will develop their awareness of the world around them whilst supporting their balance and coordination.

WHO still recommends no screen time for children under 2 at all. Once a child has turned 2, they recommend a maximum of 1-hour screen time per day, stating less is better.

36+ months

Children who are 3 and 4 should still have no more than 1 hour of screen time per day (WHO); however, the most recent Ofcom report "Children and Parents Media use Attitudes" survey published in March 2022 states that 17% of 3- and 4-year olds have their own mobile phone so there is a chance that these children are exposed to much more screen time than the recommended limit.

Some exciting and engaging technology that is more appropriate for this age group includes remote controlled vehicles, metal detectors, voice recorders, toy tills, and cameras. By this age, children are more able to use the equipment independently and will want adults around to share what they have discovered and created with the tools you have provided. These toys help with the development of fine motor skills, collaboration, and social skills and can be used to build language skills.

The early years and technology across the four nations of the UK and beyond

EYFS England

This book uses the English EYFS as its main focus mainly because this is the system I have worked with; however, many of you will be curious about how what I've written fits into the curriculum in your home nation and beyond. Here's a short overview.

Northern Ireland

The early years guidance for funded settings in Northern Ireland is similar to that used in England, which is divided into six areas of learning. The world around us is the section where technology is included. During the section in the guidance about the learning environment, technology is talked about positively and encouraged to form part of the resources available as long as they are meaningful and have a purpose. (ICT is the term used in this document); https://www.education-ni.gov.uk/articles/curricular-guidance

Wales

The early years curriculum in Wales was updated in 2022 following consultation with the sector and is aimed at settings with children aged 3 and over. For new guidance, see https://hwb.gov.wales/curriculum-for-wales/?_ga=2.32999294.1944670436.1661783316-1996159690.1661783316

Again it uses six areas of learning, one is called science and technology along with a digital competency framework. It's very thorough, do have a read.

For guidance for settings that are funded and non-maintained, see https://hwb.gov.wales/curriculum-for-wales/curriculum-for-funded-non-maintained-nursery-settings/ (Note that all settings registered with the Care Inspectorate Wales (CIE) need an awareness of the curriculum, even where they are not funded.)

Scotland

Launched in 2020 following a refresh of the Building the Ambition and Pre-birth to Three resources (2014), "Realising the Ambition" is a wonderful document. It is designed to be used by any professional working with children and acknowledges children are unique and develop at their own pace. They have included a section called digital technology and the young child. It acknowledges the creativity with technology and the importance of all children having access. If you are currently questioning your own approach as a practitioner, I strongly recommend a read. https://education.gov.scot/media/3bjpr3wa/realisingtheambition.pdf

Our neighbours in the Republic of Ireland

With a strong emphasis on play, the guidance produced for settings working with children aged 0–6 years in Ireland is thorough. However, although technology does get mentioned, it is in the context of assistive technology and there is no great emphasis on it beyond that use. You can read the full guidance here https://curriculumonline.ie/Early-Childhood/ https://ncca.ie/media/4029/aistear-they-early-childhood-curriculum-framework.pdf

Reflective prompts – How technology supports the CofEL and areas of learning

- Consider your own curriculum, how does technology fit into each area of learning?

- What characteristics of effective learning do you see children demonstrate through their interaction with technology?

This is WHO's guidelines on physical activity, sedentary behaviour, and sleep where the information about screen time came from for this chapter. (https://apps.who.int/iris/bitstream/handle/10665/311664/9789241550536-eng.pdf?sequence=1&isAllowed=y)

Conclusion

This chapter has set out how the use of technology firmly links to the statutory framework in England and offers ways that practitioners can maximise that.

It explores how technology can support the development of the characteristics of learning and all of the prime and specific areas of learning. It makes links to the age and stage of the child and clearly points out the safety risk of screen time especially for very young children.

It closes with a short section on how technology links to the curriculums in our neighbours around the UK and in the Republic of Ireland to ensure wherever you are practicing you can make the case for technology with the early years.

3 How Can We Make the Most of the Technology We Already Have?

Do you have technology toys lurking in cupboards or up on high shelves no longer used because you have not replaced the batteries, or the lead has been lost? Items sitting around, taking up space, collecting dust, unloved, and unused? This chapter will encourage you to get them down, dust them off, and reintroduce them to your space.

The joy and pleasure of being in control of a piece of equipment is immeasurable for a child. The freedom to determine at what point an object is on or off, to have that control when so much is controlled for them can be empowering and all-consuming for a young child. They can spend several minutes simply flicking a switch and wondering at the simplicity of it. So, giving them opportunities to do this is vital for you as a practitioner. It's a part of our joy to give them that control over a tiny part of their world, whenever it is possible and safe to do so.

The obvious way to do this is to ensure that the technological equipment is available, to hand and accessible to the children, so that they can make the choice to use it or not. So often I have seen "expensive" technology toys out of reach of the children and only brought out when an adult can oversee its use. I understand the reservations, budgets are tighter than ever, but if we only value equipment based on its financial cost, we and importantly the children will miss out on lots of opportunities. When a piece of equipment is accessible for free choice by the children, some will want to use it, to play with it. Some will still not be interested, but perhaps on seeing the technology becoming more usual in the setting, their interest will be piqued and they may explore equipment they would not have done before. Sometimes seeing an adult using a piece of equipment will encourage interest but for

DOI: 10.4324/9781003023173-4

some children it is less interesting than something being used independently by another child. Another good reason to have the equipment fully accessible and in reach.

In this chapter, you will find information on some of the technology that is likely to be in your setting already and may have been forgotten, reminding you of ways you can make use of those things and inspire children. I have created a template for risk assessment for some of these items which I hope will help your planning and support you recommissioning this equipment back into daily play.

Let's start by look at some of the equipment you are already likely to have access to in your setting.

Torches

A simple off/on torch can be fascinating for a child. The control of the switch, the lighting up, the shining on objects, of pointing up under the chin to put their face into shadow, all wonderful. The type of torch and the way it is powered matters little. So, if you have wind-up torches, battery powered torches, solar powered torches, or rechargeable torches, the delight and opportunities for play and learning are almost endless. Children can use a torch to make things clearer, to light up dens, to examine objects more closely, or to create an atmosphere for their storytelling. It can become a spotlight during a performance or a "secret" light whilst reading in a cosy corner. For some children, it will become a Lightsaber and depending on what your policy says about weapon play, you may encourage this (or not). Learning about cause and effect in such a simple way can be powerful and effective especially at an early stage of learning.

Remote-controlled vehicles

I loved these as a child and so do many children. For young children, I think there is an element of control and joy in making something move without touching it. Making something move quickly, slow down, and of course bang into other things (and people) is fun. Of course, they are also learning lots too. The cause and effect message is clear but there are also opportunities for learning about direction and directional language, about speed and stopping, and lots of practice for hand-eye-coordination. Figure 3.1 shows children looking at an image they have captured.

Figure 3.1 Two children sitting on a bench, looking at an image on a digital camera.

Light box

A light box allows children to explore a world of objects with an up-light that lights up the objects, creates shadows, and encourages the exploration of shapes and patterns. Having spent just a few moments searching the internet, I have discovered you can very easily and cheaply make your own. Some of the objects that could be explored using the light box are "found" objects, the objects that children collect and find around them such as feathers, leaves, seeds, and so on. Fruit slices fresh and dried can look effective giving different effects and can open a range of discussions with children. Anything with a level of transparency that allows some light through, so paper doilies, ribbons, netting, tissue paper, bottles, beads, sequins, buttons, paperclips, and of course there are specific sets of toys you can purchase for this purpose too. A light box is a technology but I think the real learning will come out of the sustained shared thinking that happens around the technology with a skillful adult alongside the child. The rich language opportunities are endless with this equipment simply because of the wonder and joy it can spark for us as well as the children.

Stopwatches/Digital timers

The item synonymous with a sports field, or the kitchen, can give children some real independence in their play and support their developing understanding of turn taking. I have seen children use timers in their play such as using it as a pretend "watch" or "clock" even when they are unable to "read" the numbers which shows a great understanding of their purpose and an early understanding of time. They can be used as an actual timer for children to see how long things take, how fast they can do something, or to wait for their turn with a piece of equipment. These things have been modelled by others around them and the children will be copying the use even without full understanding, exploring, and recreating to help them make sense of the objects. Again, there will be opportunities for language to be added into the play and for exploration and investigations into numbers, time, and measuring.

Walkie-talkies

Fiona calling, do you receive me? Come in. This simple piece of equipment can provide lots of fun and can really encourage children to develop their communication where other tools might not. The two-way communication without having to see the other person, or even be in the same room, could provide safety for a child feeling nervous, shy, or uncomfortable talking with others or putting their voice "out there" into the world. It can help to create a new way of communicating that can fit with a new role in the world of imagination and role play for children. Adults can model how to use them safely and together; you can create a code for using them. How to signal you have finished speaking for example or have understood the message? This in turn could lead to some meaningful mark-making too.

Camera

Lots of children may not have seen an actual camera and if asked might say that a camera only exists when it is integrated into their parents' mobile phone, but we know they do exist and are a wonderful resource. Being able to use a camera (not connected to another device) will provide freedom to the child. They enable children to capture their own viewpoint on the world see Figure 3.1, evidence of their hours of work in the sand tray, or images of themselves and friends playing together Figure 3.2 shows just that. Children will take unexpected images from angles and heights we have not thought of and literally give us the child's eye view of the world. Their images show us how they see the world.

Audio recording devices (Dictaphones)

Lots of adults have a real discomfort at the idea of hearing their own voice (let alone seeing themselves on screen) but children get a thrill from hearing their own voice and that of those around them. So, providing equipment that will record audio will enable this. Simple push button devices with simple record and playback options work best and if it looks like a microphone children will understand instantly where to direct their voice. Even simpler are the talking buttons, where touching the coloured button will allow for recording or playback and can be used to capture words, short sentences, or quality questions from the practitioner.

Games consoles

I imagine lots of people reading this will think I have lost my senses by even suggesting this one but they can bring a lot of benefits to the child's experience. The first one we had at home was a Sega Megadrive (unless you count

Figure 3.2 A child aged 5 taking a photograph.

the Spectrum ZX, which I do but many do not as it worked in a different way). Hours were spent (wasted) on trying to get Sonic the Hedgehog to the end of his adventure to battle Doctor Eggman collecting jewels along the way. Games consoles and "gaming" has come a long way and those that encourage more kinetic and physical play like the Wii can add something new to the setting. Not all of them have to be connected to the internet, you can use one that relies on loading the games locally to avoid that potential challenge (see Chapter 7). You can use a screen the setting already owns such as an interactive whiteboard or television and quite likely, if you ask around staff and families, someone will have a console they no longer use and will happily donate so it can be a relatively low-cost option too. It would be wise to have staff play the games first, so some teambuilding opportunities too as many games require players to work together.

CD player/Cassette player

If you still have a cassette player somewhere, hold onto it, it might be an antique soon or they might make a comeback, there were glimmers of that happening in 2020. CD players too – they seem to be dying out and disappearing but can hold great fascination for children. Again, these items can be controlled by the child, they can decide if and when it plays, skip tracks or fast forward sections, rewind to the bit they like best, stop it, and alter the volume. When I was working as a deputy manager of a nursery, that nursery was taken over by a large chain and the manager had left. I had to welcome and show round the area manager. Introduce her to staff and children and talk about how things operated. We entered the 2–3s room to find a small group of children were squealing with delight at their new "toy." They had unravelled the tape from a cassette and were spinning and winding it around objects and fully engaged in the activity. I went over to remove the tape and, in my eyes, make it safe. The area manager said stop, look at the learning going on, let them play. We watched for a few moments and she commented on their play and learning; I learnt a lot too. So there is another potential use for the tapes … just hope you are not the one having to get the pencil out …

Programmable toys (such as Bee-Bots)

When these first appeared, everyone seemed to buy one or something similar and they are a lot of fun, with massive amounts of learning opportunities for early coding. They are bright, bold, and easy to use, with a key objective of developing early coding skills. There are opportunities for directional language to be used too and they come in lots of designs and with varying accessories to extend and develop the learning further. I mentioned that when they first appeared, everyone seemed to buy one but I wonder how often yours is still used? Does it still work? Need new batteries or charging? Can you introduce it to the children and model how it works for them to have a go?

Overhead projector (OHP) old style

When I did my teacher training course, I had to prepare and deliver a micro-teach and was advised to use a tool and a topic that was new to me, to provide me with a challenge. At the time, every classroom in the college had an overhead projector (OHP) in the corner of the room and I'd not used one, so that was my tool, seriously, my challenge was to use an OHP. I taught my class the football offside rule. I was able to create a pitch that everyone could see and then move my "players" (coloured sweets) around to demonstrate the rule. Within a year of this lesson, I had an interactive white-board in my classroom, there is a tipping point for you. So, do you have an overhead projector? If your setting is attached to a school, likely there will be one somewhere so see if you can borrow it. You will need a few acetates too and pens that will write on them. You can model to the children how they work and then challenge them to create images to project to the room or see what other ways they can come up with to use the equipment. Puppet shows and storytelling are two ways you can utilise the OHP.

Metal detectors

Searching, hunting, exploring, discovering, unearthing, finding, digging, scraping, and cleaning-up. How is that for developing the characteristics of effective learning? A simple tool that just "detects" metal under things. You do not even have to add things to be found, there is a good chance there will be stuff to discover already there ... how amazing is that? Also, you can hide things in advance if you want to. Let us create the future detectorists, archae-ologists, and historians. Metal detectors that have been designed for children are smaller and some are similar in size to a torch, some will be longer and look more like the item we imagine when we think of a metal detector. Have some charged and ready for use in the garden, having buried some metal items such as toy cars or keys, or put some in the sand tray with pre-hidden coins.

Tablets

These are possibly the one item that is out and being used already but what are you doing with it? It is possible staff are using it for observations and tracking (I love this, I know this is saving time and paper). It is also possible that children have access to one or more tablets for their own use. Figure 3.3 shows a child using a tablet. They might be using the camera, the internet, or accessing apps for drawing, recording their voices or making videos, playing a range of games, watching content, connecting with others ... the list is endless here. Simply by scrolling through the app store you will find a whole range of resources that can be used by and with children. The integrated timer and stopwatch, music players and cameras are all useful tools and you can find yoga or other exercise classes can be shared. There are apps for writing and drawing, looking back at photos of

Figure 3.3 A 2-year-old boy engaged in an activity on a tablet.

their friends and things they have done in the past, measuring things, and creating fun and silly images too (apps like Boomerang).

Calculators

Just for sums? In fact, rarely for that in the early years. These small number machines become so many things for children as well as being a great way for children to engage with numbers. A "controller" for anything including people, a phone or other communication device, something to take notes on … and of course the cause and effect of pushing a button and the displaying showing it. Number recognition, symbols have meaning and lots of mathematical language can be introduced with a calculator.

Talking books

That is, books with buttons that provide sound effects and key words or even the full text as children turn the pages and press the button. Not much can beat sitting with a favoured adult, curling up, and enjoying being read to as young child but these are a good resource that can provide other learning opportunities and enable some independence too.

Interactive Whiteboard (IWB)

I mentioned these above very briefly, they have been around a long time and in some settings, they are sitting fixed to the wall and rarely get turned on anymore ... why? Sometimes because the pens have been lost or there is some minor damage to the screen, sometimes because they have realised it has been put up too high for the children. Can you overcome these challenges and bring the interactive whiteboard back into service? As long as the IWB is low enough for children to access, there is lot they can do with this. In essence, it is like having a large wall-mounted tablet. One of the main benefits with them is that children can play alongside each other on a game, a puzzle, mark-making, or storytelling. They can watch videos, play music, and it can display a backdrop for role play.

MP3 player

Downloading and playing music and stories, simply.

Visualiser

In many ways similar to the OHP we discussed earlier in the chapter, but alongside that, you can record in real time what is being shared as they have an integrated webcam too. You can show off work, share stories at a larger scale, children can display their work, you can do real-time demonstrations of drawing and writing ...

Television

Yes, there was a TV in my first nursery, we were only allowed to show videos on it (nothing as transmitted) and only if: the weather was really bad, it was the afternoon we were short on staff and we only had a few children and only for a maximum of 30 minutes. I may misremember that, but I know we only got the TV out about twice a year. I'm not sure what the reservation was about it being available more but I do know that we need to be aware of what we allow children to watch and that it is a shared experience, we can and should talk to children about what they are watching and answer their questions. The choice is wide and varied now and it is sensible to use pre-recorded rather than live transmission programmes as you can be certain of what is being shared. Again, it is useful for staff to have seen the programme in advance and be familiar with the themes and content so they are ready for the discussion that follows.

Karaoke machine

Really... it is the sort of things that lots of people bought or were given as family presents and now sits in a cupboard not being used, except maybe on special occasions (just me?). If you have one, get it out, dust it off, and set it up. Obviously check the discs and microphones still work and that the tracks provided are suitable (age appropriate). It is possible to still get discs for lots of machines, and if you have one that uses MP3 files then it is even easier to access the music. Then, load it up and see what happens. Children love using a microphone, love singing along to tunes, they may well start to create dance routines too and have backing singers and so on.

Tinker table (old equipment)

An old toaster, an obsolete mobile phone, an unused lamp ... anything that can be taken apart with screwdrivers can provide hours of thoughtful exploration. Learning about how things come apart, go back together, and maybe what makes them work. Remove the plugs first to ensure they cannot be plugged in! Modelling is useful here and mindful supervision, we should resist the urge to interfere. There will be lots of opportunities to introduce rich language and experience sustained shared thinking with the children as they explore.

Outdated tech for role play

A selection of familiar but non-working devices, such as mobile phones, kettles, remote controllers, can be used by children in their role play. Add them to your resource box for the home corner and children will be able to handle and use the objects in all sorts of ways. They will of course still make their own versions of these things, depending on the play they are engaged with, but it is another option for exploring their world.

Risk assessment

You are well aware of the importance of risk assessment and doing this before introducing new equipment is essential, this is especially true when the equipment is old or not been used for some time. By completing a risk assessment, you will be able to identify the benefits and drawbacks on re/introducing the item and make an informed decision about whether to or not.

To support you in this process you will find an example risk assessment on the next few pages; it is not intended to replace your own processes but to prompt and support your own risk assessment procedures. It is a sample which you should build on for your own environment and children. Please note: not all of the equipment listed has been "risk-assessed" here.

Resources/ Equipment	Hazards	Risk level	Who is at risk?	What measures are already in place?	What else can you do to reduce the risk?	Risk level	Who will do this?	Date for review
Torches – wind-up, battery powered, solar powered, and rechargeable (mains charge)	Electrical fault Overheating Using as a weapon Shining lights in eyes	Low	Children and staff	Only items that meet British safety standards are provided in the setting Each item visually checked weekly Guidance for children around safe use displayed and shared by staff Rechargeable torches only charged over night	Modelling use of the torches will help children understand safe use. Encourage children to create the safety rules with you.	Low	All staff	
Radio-controlled vehicles	Electrical fault Battery leak Interfering with others' play Trip hazard	Low	Children and Staff	Only items that meet British safety standards are provided in the setting Each item visually checked before use An area is defined for their use to reduce trip hazard and to show others where it is safer for them to be	Playing alongside children so that modelling can used to as a teaching method.	Low	All staff	

(Continued)

Resources/ Equipment	Hazards	Risk level	Who is at risk?	What measures are already in place?	What else can you do to reduce the risk?	Risk level	Who will do this?	Date for review
Light-box	Looking directly into the light; Glass breaking	Low	Children and Staff	Used with an adult supervising (not controlling); Reminders about safety given to children before and during use; Only items that meet British safety standards are provided in the setting; Each item visually checked before use	Simple rules around use	Low	All staff	
Stopwatches/ Digital timers	Small batteries – choke hazard; Lanyard – strangling hazard	Low	Children and Staff	Only items that meet British safety standards are provided in the setting; Each item visually checked weekly; Safety lanyards only – those with quick release to be used.; Ensure battery compartment is sealed	Make them easily accessible and have enough available for multiple use	Low	All staff	

(Continued)

Resources/ Equipment	Hazards	Risk level	Who is at risk?	What measures are already in place?	What else can you do to reduce the risk?	Risk level	Who will do this?	Date for review
Walkie-talkie	Heavy – weapon potential Connecting to external channels	Low	Children and Staff	Only items that meet British safety standards are provided in the setting Each item visually checked weekly Reminders of safe use with children Closed channels so they can only be used internally. Single channel and close range devices are best for nursery use.	Model their use with children, have additional resources that show how they can be used	Low	All staff	
Camera	Taking inappropriate images such as in the bathroom Small battery – choke hazard Strap – strangling hazard	Low	Children and staff	Only items that meet British safety standards are provided in the setting Each item visually checked weekly Clear rules around safe use shared with children Clear signage – no photos here for any areas where it is not appropriate such as toilets, sleep area, the office.	Modelling their use, make them accessible to all Remove strap if possible, or ensure it has a safety quick release	Low	All staff	

(Continued)

Resources/ Equipment	Hazards	Risk level	Who is at risk?	What measures are already in place?	What else can you do to reduce the risk?	Risk level	Who will do this?	Date for review
Recording devices	Recording conversations not for children – safeguarding; Playback - Sound – loud, ear damage	Low	Children and staff	If the device has capability, set volume limits, provide headphones for playback, Clear signage for where you can record, Clear rules for safe use with children	Model using a voice recorder and open discussions about when and why we might record	Low	All staff	
Games consoles	Leads – trip and strangling hazard; Flicking screen – could cause seizures; Sound – loud, ear damage	Low	Children and staff	Screen time should be limited for all children so limit availability of console; Ensure only age appropriate content on games; Limit volume and provide headphones; Ensure quality of screen to reduce flicking	Model how to use, check content ahead of providing for children	Low	All staff	
CD player/ Cassette player	Fingers trapped in machine; Tape unravelling – trip and strangling hazard; Sound – loud, ear damage	Low	Children and staff	An adult to demonstrate to child on first use; Adult supervision; Children to be given clear guidance	Headphones to be provided but used with supervision to limit volume to a safe level	Low	All staff	

(Continued)

Resources/ Equipment	Hazards	Risk level	Who is at risk?	What measures are already in place?	What else can you do to reduce the risk?	Risk level	Who will do this?	Date for review
Projector	Bright light Large equipment – heavy – falling	Low	Children and staff	It is fixed to a stand that is only accessible by an adult Children given clear guidance about not looking directly at the light	Look into having it fixed to the wall	Low	All staff	
Metal detectors	Finding dangerous items in the ground such as contaminated litter	Medium	Children and staff	The area used with the detectors has been checked by staff The detectors are only strong enough to "detect" below surface level	Children encouraged to share their treasures with an adult and ask them to dig them out of the ground	Low	Staff	
Tablets	Accessing the internet – inappropriate content	Medium	Children and staff	Software installed on all devices that restricts content Children encouraged to share what they do online with adults	Children know what to do if they see something that makes them uncomfortable	Low	Staff	
Calculators	Small batteries – choking hazard	Medium	Children	Ensure the batteries are secure Visual checks each day		Low	Staff	

(Continued)

Resources/ Equipment	Hazards	Risk level	Who is at risk?	What measures are already in place?	What else can you do to reduce the risk?	Risk level	Who will do this?	Date for review
Tinker Table	Screwdrivers, plugs, small parts	Low	Children and staff	All items checked regularly Supervision Very small parts removed	Modelling of how to use equipment by staff	Low	Staff	
Old-tech	Plugs/cables, small parts, heavy	Low	Children and staff	As tinker table Ensure fuses are removed to ensure items cannot be plugged in or 'live' Heavier items can be set up on the floor or lower table		Low	Staff	

Risk assessing is a skill that we all use frequently throughout the day even when we are not necessarily "risk assessing" and is a skill that we can build on. To put it simply, to assess a risk is to judge how likely an injury will occur from doing the thing you are assessing and if injury does occur, how bad might it be. So, if you are planning a short trip to the woods with a group of toddlers, one risk you will identify is trip hazards – things like tree roots, rocks, mounds of earth (leaves), etc. It is very likely at least one child will trip, it is also likely that that trip will result in a low level of injury, such as a graze, small bump, or cut to the knee. So, it is highly likely to occur, but with a low injury this would mean we should risk assess this hazard as low risk and with a few simple measures we could reduce that further. We would certainly consider this a safe activity and it would go ahead. The measures might include an adult going ahead and planning a route through the woods where some of these obstacles could be reduced or avoided, you would have a higher ratio of adults to ensure supervision and you would remind the children about safe exploration of the space. You would ensure safe footwear and appropriate clothing; all of these are measures that help to reduce the risk further.

Sometimes we are required to write down risk assessments, such as a trip to the woods, but sometimes it is more instinctive and dynamic. In your setting, you'll find written risk assessments for the building, for areas in and around the building, for security of the premises, for storing cleaning products, for pieces of equipment, for who comes into the building, and lots more. You should be familiar with these as they will have an impact on your role, and when you get a new piece of equipment or are planning for something "out of the ordinary," you might be asked to produce a written risk assessment. Even if you are not, you need to be an effective assessor of risk to work with children.

Consider this

As children arrive, a parent hands you a bag as they are leaving and says "thought the children might like playing with these, they don't work anymore."

You put the bag to one side, and once the children are in and playing, you take a look inside.

There is a selection of old electrical and battery operated items such as a remote control, a toaster, and a radio.

How do you risk assess the equipment and what might you do with it next?

During the day, we risk assess constantly, noticing when the floor is becoming too cluttered, or when children are becoming more boisterous in their play. We find ways to reduce the risk while ensuring children can continue in their play. We make things as safe as necessary for this to happen.

It is a skill that becomes ingrained, and we do it without conscious thought. I have often been heard to share that I do this when out in a group, head-counting my friends/family, even adult only groups, to ensure we have not lost anyone. It has become instinctive and wanting to keep others safe is a good quality to have.

Reflective prompts

Once you have carried out your audit, it might be useful to consider the following:

- Do you use your existing technology effectively with the children?

- Do children have access to the technology? How can you make it more accessible?

- What barriers are in place that restrict the equipment's use and how can these be overcome?

Conclusion

I hope through your reading of this chapter you will have rediscovered technology equipment that had been relegated to the back of the cupboard long ago and that this has helped to spark a new way of using and looking at how you can incorporate technology into the day within your setting. I hope it has also sparked a new interest for the children and that they have explored, played, imagined new ways of using the equipment and playing together with technology. I imagine, they may have taught you a few things too. You might also have found some items that had been put away that had stopped working and have been able to repair them, recharge them, or add new batteries to give them a new lease of life.

4 New Technology

I have mentioned already that technology is not going anywhere, the year 2020 and all that it brought with it confirmed that with so many of us relying on technology for learning, for work, for connecting; it is also evolving at a rapid rate. If you feel you cannot keep up or are not sure what is next, some of the resources in this chapter might make your head spin. Alternatively, you might feel excited about what the future (already here) can offer your children.

In this chapter, I describe pieces of technology that emerged in the last few years or that may not have been considered by your team for use within an early years setting. Some of these things might seem too "sci-fi" to be real but they do all exist and are being used in a range of ways across different industries. Some of the devices are not designed with children in mind or it is not initially obvious as something to engage children with but they can be adapted. Of course, some of the technology is already a part of the child's world in their homes and so having the opportunity to help them interact safely and appropriately is an important part of our work.

I provide a brief explanation of the resource and then some suggestions of how it could be used with and by young children. Although some of these items are pricey and often beyond a typical early years setting budget, there are often cheaper alternatives so I've included some ideas about to get access to some of these items.

Smart speaker (Echo, Siri, Google home, etc.)

What is it? A device that is connected to the internet and responds to voice controls. You can play music, get answers to questions such as what time the supermarket will open and what will the weather be like today, and play games.

DOI: 10.4324/9781003023173-5

These began to appear in homes, cafes, pubs, everywhere from 2014 and are a lot of fun as well as really useful devices for lots of reasons. Being voice activated means you can operate them without needing to read or write, which is great for young children. Many children will be familiar with them and know how to operate them, knowing the command word means anyone can get the device to play certain tracks or respond to questions. Security is important (see more in Chapter 7) but so is talking with children about how to use them safely and modelling safe and appropriate use as a staff team too. Children can be independent in such things as researching a topic or choosing a piece of music to move to. To work it does need to be connected to the internet so make sure you check the security settings and parental controls to minimise the risk of children accessing inappropriate content.

A smart speaker is great for children with emerging language or those who struggle to use a tablet or keyboard.

Telepresence robot

What is it? A robot connected to a tablet via the internet, transmitting live from your classroom (or anywhere the robot is allowed in) enabling those not with you to see, hear, and interact with your session. A child at home with a tablet, connects to the robot and can move it around the space to see what is going on and is able to ask questions and interact with the others in the classroom. They have been pioneered in hospital schools and helped to keep children connected whilst being treated for and recovering from long-term illnesses and accidents. Children enjoy being a part of the "usual" daily life of the school and getting to see their teachers and friends.

How could this be useful to early years? I think this could be especially useful for children joining the setting for the first time as part of the settling in process, enabling children to see the setting and people from the safety of their own home. This could be especially useful if a family is moving to the area and so the settling in period may be shorter than preferred, the settling in could start before the child moves into the area. As with the hospital schools, a child being off for a period of time due to illness could keep in touch with their friends and key person, join in with story time, and be involved in role play. After a child has left the setting, they could use the robot to keep in touch with the setting, particularly useful for any child struggling with the transition away from the setting.

Smart hub

What is it? A device connected to various appliances around a building for remote control, even when away from the building. This includes such things as heating and lighting, adjusting temperature, boiling a kettle, or closing blinds.

It is not uncommon to see an adult give a child the privilege of being the one to turn off the lights before movie time, or pressing the button at the crossing, and a smart hub can be used in the same way. In general, children do not play with the light switches in the setting as they recognise it is not a toy and the smart hub can be given the same level of responsibility. In turn, this can give a child some control over the environment which is usually outside of a child's realm but with a smart hub they can contribute, lighting, heating, anything that is Wi-Fi connected. It can be a great conversation starter too, imagine the questions children will have about how the device works.

Time-lapse camera

What is it? A camera that takes many photos over a long period and then replays them at a quicker speed to show progress of the thing it was photographing. It is possible to get the same effect using a smartphone or tablet and downloading an app that works in the same way.

Creating a time-lapse video or series of images gives us the ability to see slow changes more quickly, such as growing seeds, the sun setting, clouds moving, a cake baking (rising), and a child growing. It could be used to make a movie that can look very funny on playback because of the "stilted" or "jumping" figures; this can be great for discussions around experimenting and trial and error approaches to things, why did that happen? What could we do to change it? And so on.

As the camera takes images at set times, it does not require someone to press the shutter, so a child can "instruct" an adult or other child, how to set it up, where to position it, and how often to take an image. This means any child who struggles to manipulate the camera can still be involved in using it.

Motion sensor camera

Each time something triggers the camera it records, useful for such things as security but could be interesting for children too. The main benefit of a motion sensor camera is that it only records when there is something happening. This would be great if your setting was experiencing nocturnal visitors in the grounds such as a hedgehog, or if you have nesting box, you could set it up to watch the comings and goings of the birds as they feed their young and watch them grow.

In a similar way to the time-lapse camera, this can be used by children without the need to manipulate the device. Once it is set up, they can move in front of it to trigger the shutter, place objects in front of the lens, and so on.

Body camera

A camera is worn on the body, either with a harness across the chest or on the head. These are often used for extreme sports and by emergency service personnel, but I am sure they could be fun and interesting for children too. A body camera could provide a child's eye view of the world like nothing else, even if only for a snapshot of time which would allow us, the practitioners, to learn about their world in a different way, from a different perspective. I wonder what the children would make of the replay.

Activity trackers

Usually worn on the wrist like a watch, these are used to record movement and more advanced trackers can record other body measures such as heart rate. Many do also tell the time. Increasingly, we are seeing children wearing these and at a younger age but could we have some in the setting? The opportunity to notice how far you travel, how you breath, your heart beats, all great learning opportunities for children in terms of simple biology, through to learning about healthy living. Could there be an element of competition amongst the children (and staff) for distance travelled in a set time or perhaps to encourage that child who prefers to sit and rarely moves around the setting to encourage, for a short period of time, to move around.

Microscopes

A piece of equipment that enables us to closely examine objects, especially those we have discovered. Everyday objects under a microscope can look almost alien and can provide some wonderful learning about how things are made or created. The microscope can be used to help identify leaves, plants, and bugs discovered in the garden by getting really close to be sure of just how many legs it has or if the petals are pointy or curved. Science and discovery learning is accompanied by lots of rich language.

Talking pegs

These are simple devices that can be used to make audio recordings. Voices, real-world noises, music, and so on. They come in various lengths of "track" and play back instantly. You can use them to record key words for children to hear when playing with certain equipment or children can capture stories they are telling friends, you might use them to pose a question in the construction area that children can listen to and respond to in their play or children might use them to record their conversations or funny words.

3D and 4D projectors

These are quite specialist and expensive but do provide another opportunity to play and learn with technology. These projectors can be ceiling or wall mounted and project anything from a flower bed to an underwater world to explore. Depending on the software, you can play football, run through flowers, follow a trail, count monkeys, swim with fishes, or almost anything else your imagination can think of.

Illuminated whiteboards

An illuminated whiteboard is a simple idea – a screen lit from behind. They come in a range of sizes so can be handheld or laid on a tabletop or floor. I've seen them used mostly for mark making and the colours can often be changed to create different effects while the child creates or once they have finished; I've also seen children use them as a scene creator for small world play which of course can be ever changing.

Colour changing toys

These provide a sensory experience whilst also providing other play and learning. For example, a simple colour changing ball can be used for rolling (physical), enjoying the colour changes (sensory) and talking about the movement of the ball (KW) as well as providing time to play 1:1 with an adult or another child and build connection (PSE).

Sensory light boxes/tubes

A change in the light or colour of light in a space can affect the mood of the child by creating a calmer atmosphere for them to be in. It can also change the atmosphere to one that sparks creativity and energy so requires careful planning. A lightbox can have items placed onto it for exploring how the light and colour changes the objects and comes through, this can simply be used as a quiet, relaxing time or to extend a child's understanding of some scientific concepts.

Virtual Reality (VR) headsets

Included here not to recommend their use but to provide a word of caution.

A VR headset is a device usually worn on the head (some smaller versions are hand-held) and connect to software or the Wi-Fi to show "real" experiences such as exploring the bottom of the ocean or flying an airplane. It can provide a chance to experience another world, both real and imagined and often one beyond our wildest dreams. They have been designed for adults and teens and there is little research about using them with children under the age of 8, the little research that is available though does find some positive reasons for young children to engage in using VR but it has not been widely tested to ensure safety for this age group. Concerns include such things as potential impact on vision and balance stability as well as children not being able to fully distinguish between fantasy and reality.

I am not suggesting that settings go out and buy a VR headset (even if they do have the funds) but my purpose for mentioning it here is that as they become more mainstream children may well have access to them at home. Older siblings, parents, extended family and friends may have them and use them so knowing about them, how they are used, and to keep children safe is useful for us as practitioners.

Risk assessment

New equipment must always be risk assessed before allowing the children access so once again you will find a template including some of the equipment I've talked about here. Remember this is a starting point and should not replace your own risk assessment processes. I hope it is helpful for pieces of equipment you are less familiar with and by completing the risk assessment you will learn a bit more about each piece of equipment, which in turn will help you to support the children. A risk assessment is not just about the equipment, you need to consider the space it is being used in, the people you have operating it, and the skills they have as well as individual needs of everyone who is in the setting.

Risk assessment samples

Resources/ Equipment	Hazards	Risk level	Who is at risk?	What measures are already in place?	What else can you do to reduce the risk?	Risk level	Who will do this?	Date to be in place by?
Telepresence robots	Trip hazard as they move around the space, electricals – so keep away from water. Connection to Wi-Fi and therefore could be open to being hacked	Low	Children and staff in the room. The setting	All electrical equipment is subject to PAT as per HSE guidelines (https://www.hse.gov.uk/electricity/faq-portable-appliance-testing.htm) annually. All Wi-Fi enabled devices have security in place as does the Wi-Fi connection. Equipment is store securely and away from other hazards such as water. Permissions of all those present in the room obtained and stored as anyone in the room could appear on the screen	Training for the staff and talking to the children about safe use of the device. Display simple rules about how to interact with it and staff to model this	Low	All staff	

(Continued)

Resources/ Equipment	Hazards	Risk level	Who is at risk?	What measures are already in place?	What else can you do to reduce the risk?	Risk level	Who will do this?	Date to be in place by?
Smart hubs	Wires electronics Wi-Fi connection	Medium	Children and staff in the room	All electrical equipment is subject to PAT as per HSE guidelines (https://www.hse. gov.uk/electricity/faq-portable-appliance-testing.htm) annually All Wi-Fi enabled devices have security in place as does the Wi-Fi connection Device stored with wires hidden to avoid trips	Training for the staff and talking to the children about safe use of the device Display simple rules about how to interact with it and staff to model this	Low	All staff	
Time-lapse and motion sense cameras	Privacy Security	Low	Children and staff, families, public	The location of the devices must not capture images in places where privacy can be assumed such as private gardens, bathrooms and areas used for changing They should not capture images of members of the public such as on streets or car parks Permission should be obtained to share images captured	Training for the staff and talking to the children about safe use of the device Display simple rules about how to interact with it and staff to model this	Low	Staff	

(Continued)

Resources/ Equipment	Hazards	Risk level	Who is at risk?	What measures are already in place?	What else can you do to reduce the risk?	Risk level	Who will do this?	Date to be in place by?
Body cam	Privacy Security	Low	Children and staff	Permission should be sought from all children in the space where the body cam will be worn Permission should be sought to share images captured	Training for the staff and talking to the children about safe use of the device Staff should monitor the use of the device and ensure it is worn safely	Low	Staff	
Activity trackers	Permissions, data capture allergy to material on skin	Low	Children and staff	Permission should be sought for some data capture and sharing such as any personal information; if only counting steps this would not be necessary Use devices that can be worn over clothing such as a sleeve to avoid being directly against the skin	Training for staff in how to use the data captured sensitively and sharing with the children how to use the tracker safely	Low	Staff	

(Continued)

Resources/ Equipment	Hazards	Risk level	Who is at risk?	What measures are already in place?	What else can you do to reduce the risk?	Risk level	Who will do this?	Date to be in place by?
Microscopes	Glass components could be vulnerable to damage The lights used are strong so could cause short term damage to eyes (especially those of young children) The small objects placed under the microscope are a potential choke hazard if not handled correctly	Low	Children and staff	Appropriate supervision of children Limit time spent with the instrument to minimise exposure to strong light Talking to the children about safe use	Staff modelling how to use the instrument safely	Low	Staff	

(Continued)

Resources/ Equipment	Hazards	Risk level	Who is at risk?	What measures are already in place?	What else can you do to reduce the risk?	Risk level	Who will do this?	Date to be in place by?
3D and 4D projectors	Motion sickness (the projections are very lifelike) Eye damage (the bulb is strong)	Low	Children and staff	Introduce new games and visualisations slowly, encourage everyone to start on the floor and stand slowly. If someone feels unwell, get them to move away from the projections and sit quietly. Ensure no one stares directly at the bulb on the projector, they should look at the images being created	Staff modelling how to interact with the projections. Talk to the children about what will happen, what to expect, how to interact with the projections safely	Low	Staff	

(Continued)

Resources/ Equipment	Hazards	Risk level	Who is at risk?	What measures are already in place?	What else can you do to reduce the risk?	Risk level	Who will do this?	Date to be in place by?
Smart speaker (A Toniebox or Yoto might be a more child friendly option)	Access to inappropriate content Wires Security	Medium	Children and staff	Safe Search and other parental controls in place to reduce risk of inappropriate content	All electrical equipment is subject to PAT as per HSE guidelines (https://www. hse.gov.uk/ electricity/ faq-portable- appliance-testing. htm) annually All Wi-Fi enabled devices have security in place as does the Wi-Fi connection Device stored with wires hidden to avoid trips	Low	Staff	

(Continued)

Resources/ Equipment	Hazards	Risk level	Who is at risk?	What measures are already in place?	What else can you do to reduce the risk?	Risk level	Who will do this?	Date to be in place by?
Talking pegs	Batteries	Low	Children	When changing batteries ensure the casing is fixed	Supervision	Low	Staff	
Illuminated whiteboards	Could be dropped in small hands	Low	Children	Due to the shape they could be tricky for small hands so a carrier would be a good idea	Modelling how to use the device	Low	Staff	
Colour changing toys	Depends on specific device but smaller items could be 'launched'	Low	Children and staff	Modelling safe and appropriate use Talking to children about safe use – sharing rules of use		Low	Staff	
Sensory light boxes	Power cable could provide a trip hazard	Low	Children and staff	Position near to power source	If possible acquire one with a rechargeable element	Low	Staff	

Consider this: You work in the 2- to 3-year-old room and three children speak English as an additional language (they each have a different home language). You want to support their language development in English, in what ways can technology support this? What will you need to consider before using the technology you have suggested? How will you introduce the technology into their play?

Where can I get this equipment from?

Many of us don't have a budget to simply go out and buy lots of new tech but there are other ways you can access some of it. I've made suggestions in the following sections. If you find something that works, do share your local knowledge with other settings through social media and networking.

Borrowing

Firstly, a great way to try out new technology is to borrow some. You could call out to families to see if they have old or spare items you could borrow, perhaps they have something they simply don't use anymore. (They might be happy for you to keep them too.)

You could contact local settings and perhaps arrange tech swaps, what have you got that they don't and vice versa; perhaps you could arrange a swap for half a term.

Maybe you have a local lending library or Library of Things (www. libraryofthings.co.uk) and could borrow one from there.

Do you have links with your local further or higher education institution, do they have some equipment they could let you borrow? Perhaps they have students who would like to come in and demonstrate them to the staff and children. If there is an education department there, they may also have a teaching resource library. Is it possible to access this, particularly out of their term times when students don't need access to the items?

Second-Hand

Various social media sites have buy, sell, swap sites, and it is worth posting about the sort of things that you'd like to try in a local group as well as carrying out searches in these groups to see what is already being offered.

You could try:

■ Facebook marketplace along with any local selling sites on that platform.

■ Gumtree and Freecycle are used to offer items for free and have good search feature.

■ Several charities now operate an online shop such as Oxfam.

■ Apps like Shpock also list items that could be perfect.

You could try local charity shops, especially larger ones where they have space to store and safety check electrical equipment.

The local tip also often has a section for electrical items, people often discard things that work perfectly.

Car-boot sales can prove to be goldmines and local fayres often have bric-a-brac stalls which again might provide some bargains.

Sponsorship

A local business who would like to support you – a tech company or one with a public interest to support the adults of the future. Perhaps a staff member or a parent has a contact and could ask about how the business could support your setting.

Demonstration items

Large educational suppliers have a wide range of resources and these need testing – do you have connections with a rep who could provide a tech toy for your setting to try out? This is usually on the basis of your setting providing a review of the item once you've played with it.

Refurbished items

There are websites where you can buy "as new" items that have been pre-loved and then refurbished. They come with a guarantee just as a new item but are cheaper than buying new.

Buying new (the last option)

Look out for the previous model rather than the latest one of the things you want, they are often sold more cheaply. Set up a wishlist on a shopping website and send it to families and your supporters, maybe they can help you purchase something. The best tip for buying new is to shop around, check local independent suppliers as well as large online retailers to find the best price before you commit.

Safety

With all of these options especially anything second–hand, do make sure you get the items fully checked out by a suitably qualified professional before letting the children play with it and carry out a thorough risk assessment.

What to get and when to get it

It is unrealistic to think you can acquire a full range of tech items in your setting overnight so it is important to think about which tech equipment will provide the greatest impact for your setting and for the children's learning.

I suggest the first step is to carry out an audit across the whole setting to identify what technology equipment you already have access to and what learning it supports. An example follows but do create your own to suit your needs.

List of items we already have	How many?	How are they used and how to they link to learning?	How often is it used?	How accessible is the equipment for all children?
Digital camera	1	The use of the camera supports children communication, fine motor skills, hand-eye coordination, storytelling skills, creative thinking, and understanding the world.	Every day	Many of our toddlers are able to use cameras, the large viewer on the back makes it easy for one child with reduced vision to use the camera.

(Continued)

List of items we already have	How many?	How are they used and how to they link to learning?	How often is it used?	How accessible is the equipment for all children?
		The children use the images for storytelling, art and in their role play.		
Tablets	2	Children use these for searching for information on the internet, sharing videos with friends, listening to music, taking photos, and recording themselves. The children are learning about the world, building relationships, developing their language skills, and much more	Every day	The large screen makes it easy for all children to view what is on the screen, font is set larger than standard. The device is hard for smaller hands to hold so a case with handles was added.
Smart Speakers	1			

Items we'd like	How many?	Link to areas of learning	How likely would we be to use it?	
Light box	1	Generates curiosity and wonder, can be used with a range of other items including "found" items so can link to a wide range of learning areas. Will encourage communication and can lead to mark-making too.	It could be part of the continuous provision and always accessible, so frequently	All children can use this but the younger children will need adult support.

(Continued)

Items we'd like	How many?	Link to areas of learning	How likely would we be to use it?	
Motion sensor camera	1	Great for exploring night-time nature leading to communication, could also lead to researching via books and online	Could be positioned to work over night, would be used to see what had been captured, might only lead to extension activities weekly.	It is likely that this will mostly be adult led.
Activity trackers	4			

Once you have audited your equipment and made assessments about the items you'd like to add, you are in a strong position to prioritise what would provide the greatest benefit to you, the children and the setting. An audit shows you have considered options and that thought has been put into the process, which helps when asking for budget to be spent in this area too.

Action list

I encourage you to make a wishlist and consider each item in terms of what it would add to your provision.

Next, write an action plan of ways to acquire those items – get everyone involved.

Consider the pros and cons of each item.

Consider how you could convince the bill payer to buy each item.

Reflective prompts

■ Why it is important to expose children to new technologies? What might they gain from these experiences?

■ How does acquiring new technology link to the cultural capital of the setting?

Conclusion

It can feel daunting considering acquiring new equipment especially if it is a piece of technology that you are unfamiliar with and have not used yourself before, so I suggest talking to others that have. Don't restrict this to your colleagues, families once again can be a great resource here. Whatever you do and whichever approach you take, exposing children to new and different technology will broaden their experiences, expand their knowledge, and help them develop skills. They might even be able to show you how to use it.

Challenge yourself and your setting to try one new piece of technology and take it from there; enjoy the brave new frontier.

5 Technology Beyond the Setting

This chapter looks at the world around us and notices the technology that we interact with as we go about our daily lives. It also points out the ways that we can use these technologies with children and teach them how easy accessing and using technology is. How it is a part of life that enhances it and for lots of us, makes life easier. Lots of the technology around us can be used by children independently or with little "supervision" or interference from adults and as the adult, we can enrich the children's world by embracing the technology and engaging in conversations about it and its uses along with the many benefits to all.

Technology in the "real world"

We are all aware of how using a piece of equipment helps our learning of how to use and make sense of it. "How can we apply this to our work with children when we are out in the 'real' world with them?"

A large underpinning theme of Understanding of the World in the EYFS is using real-world learning to support children's development. Noticing and using the everyday and ordinary things in the child's world will provide a wealth of opportunities for learning about the technology that we use all the time, even rely on is very much a part of those learning opportunities.

So what sort of opportunities am I talking about and where is this technology? I've illustrated some in a word cloud, see Figure 5.1. Further you will find explanations of several real-world technologies many of which are already part of the child's world.

DOI: 10.4324/9781003023173-6

push-button doors

hand sanitiser dispenser

travellators

scan as you shop

escalators

ticket machines   lifts   door bells

self-checkout   dr check-in   car key fobs

weighing scales   gps   library machine

bus bells

road crossings

soap dispenser

talking rubbish bin

Figure 5.1 Word cloud for real-world technology, created by F Joines using mentimeter.

Push-button accessible doors

Since the introduction of the Disability Discrimination Act 1995, public buildings such as schools, shops, libraries, offices, and hospitals have had to ensure they are accessible to all. New buildings include this in the planning stages and many older buildings have been adapted to make accessibility easier. Automated doors are one way that buildings have become more accessible. They mostly work in one of two ways. Either with a sensor that detects a person is close and opens without need for an
y contact or doors that have a large button to press that opens it without needing to touch the door. Automated doors ensure a person who uses a wheelchair or mobility aid or someone pushing a pushchair can gain access with ease. That provides more learning, how brilliant that technology has provided a solution to a problem that many of us may not have even been aware existed until the door pads appeared. They use cause and effect as well as practical implications, and opportunities are everywhere to explore this technology.

NB: The Disability Discrimination Act 1995 was superseded by the Equality Act 2010.

Soap and sanitiser dispensers

These have been around for a long time but if you had not used them by the start of 2020, you most certainly will have done by the time you are reading this. It is another technology relying on cause and effect where you press the button with your hand or foot or hold your hand under a sensor and soap or sanitiser comes out in a measured portion. Public spaces have become filled with the sanitiser units and along with the soap dispensers in public toilets, we also see automatic taps and hand dryers. All of which are fascinating to children and provide learning.

Escalators/Travellators

I find these fun because they work without you doing anything except stepping on to them. And then they move ... all by themselves, seemingly. So, why are they included here? They provide exciting opportunities for discussion about how things work and, even if you do not know, the child will have ideas and they might well be more elaborate than the reality; it's certainly the sort of thing children are interested in. A chance to share in some imaginative play – How do they work?

Scan as you shop

If you are someone who prefers to not have to queue even for the self-check-out, you might use the supermarkets self-scan option. This is where you use a hand-held scanner to log what you put in your trolley as you shop. It can save time because you simply put everything in your trolley, scan as you go, and pay through your account. However, it also provides opportunities for children to get involved with the technology and the process of shopping. Using the scanner is simple and a child could be given this task, even if they are seated at the front of the trolley as shown in Figure 5.2. Discussion around this process could be rich and open the thinking about how the machine works and the child can watch as the numbers go up on the small screen prompting a maths conversation. It could be that by allowing a child to scan even a couple of the items, this discussion happens and leads to more questions and exploration.

Parking meters/Ticket machines

This may not be an obvious piece of technology that we would usually involve children with but when they are in a safe place such as inside the vestibule of a car park, as opposed to the side of the road, children can help with this. Following step-by-step instructions to insert the ticket, pay with coins or notes

Figure 5.2 A boy child aged 2 years helping with the shopping.

and then to listen as the machine stamps the card and releases it back to you, along with any change in a matter of moments. Again, using the machine can open up a discussion about the technology but also the larger ticket machines often display a flow diagram of how to use them and so children can follow the process as you do it. The diagram shows the process and all technology requires a process to make it work. Sometimes these machines have images as well as words so even early readers can follow the instructions.

Lifts or elevators

Lots of buildings have public lifts and if you have a pushchair, wheelchair, find stairs challenging for any reason, they ensure you can get around the whole building. Whether this is a flat where you live or a shop or somewhere you work, lifts make the place accessible. They rely on a technology that is relatively simple, so they definitely count as real-world technology.

Push the button, watch the lift progress, wait for the doors to open. Once inside, select your floor by a simple press of another button and you are transported to where you want to be. So simple in fact, a child can do this, and conversations about the lift, about numbers and direction (up and down) are all valuable, not to be missed opportunities.

Doorbells

When visiting friends and relatives on arrival at their front door, we usually need to ring the bell so they know we are there, a simple action that we may not consider a learning opportunity for children but it can be. As with many of the items discussed, cause and effect is a key aspect of technology and here when the bell is rung, someone who is usually pleased to see us, opens the door.

Self-checkouts

Despite concerns they will take jobs away from humans, self-checkouts are a popular and useful way of getting out of the supermarket quickly, unless of course you use it as an opportunity to engage any children you have with you with the technology. Young children can scan the items (see Figure 5.3), place them in the bagging area, weigh the fruit and vegetables, count quantities of loose items, and insert coins and notes into the machine (if they can reach).

All the while, there will be rich conversations between the two of you about the process, about numbers, about what you might make with the ingredients, about like and dislikes, about treats and much more. It can also be a good way to practice being patient when things do not go as planned and you have to wait for an assistant to come and confirm the item is in the bagging area or that yes in fact you do look over 25(!).

Health centre appointment screen

On arrival at the surgery it is really quick and easy to self-register and tell the doctor or nurse you have arrived for your appointment, the automated system has been used for several years now and many of us are used to it; we

Figure 5.3 A 2-year-old, girl child, checking out at the supermarket, she can reach, just!

may not even realise we have become so accustomed to the way it works. The device is very simple to use as it relies on a touchscreen meaning almost all of us can use it independently. So, even a child not yet able to read can move the screen on with an adult's help. The adult can use their finger (not on the screen but near to it) to show the child what is being asked and where to press, they can do the pressing and make the screen move on, and this shows the cause and effect in action, for a purpose.

Weighing scales in supermarkets

In the supermarkets that sell fruit and vegetables loose, they usually provide some scales so that the customer can work out how much they are buying, and therefore how much they will have to pay before putting the produce in to a bag and into their trolley. One shop local to me has a traditional set of scales that don't require a battery, but many have a digital set of scales – both types of scales are forms of technology and both can be used by children to explore how they work. Asking and answering questions about how it works as well as lots of mathematical language; heavier, lighter, all adds to the child's learning.

Bus bells

For many children, this is often one of the first opportunities to interact with technology in a safe way outside of the home, pressing the bell to ask the bus driver to stop so you can get off the bus; cause and effect. I certainly remember this experience (although, like the road crossings, my younger siblings got to press the bell more than me!).

GPS device (global positioning system)

Almost anyone with a smartphone has a GPS device (even if they do not realise it) and some people have a separate GPS device that they keep in the car for getting around without having to read a map. Both are simple to set up and use and you can involve a child in using one. Programming the device or app alongside the child, explaining what you are doing, asking them where you are going, and so on provides an opportunity to discuss the technology as well as directional language. Once it is programmed, it will give voice directions and children enjoy hearing and repeating these. It might even distract them from asking "are we there yet?"

Library self-service

Discovering the library is one of the most wonderful memories I have of child-hood; we had a small local one within walking distance of where I lived so we regularly went along to change our books. Being able to check out my own books felt very grown up but then I had to take them to the counter for the library assistant to do the stamping in the book and taking the card out to file away until the book was returned. The ability now to check out your own books with a machine is even more exciting to me (well, the first time was). The arrival of the self-checkout machines has seen the number of staff decrease but, it has meant that many of our libraries have remained and for that I am very grateful. If you have not

Figure 5.4 A child checking out a book in the library.

been to your library for a long time, I encourage you to pop in and see how they are still in many ways the same as they have always been except now they usually have an electronic machine where you scan the barcode of the book and it gets added to your account. My local library has a lovely large children's area with its own machine and I always see children scanning their own books just like in Figure 5.4 and watching for the red line to sense the barcode and then beep to show the book has registered. I also always hear rich conversations about the books and the machine "how did it do that Daddy? What does the beep mean Grandma?" and so on.

Road crossings

What a joy to be the one to press the button and make the red man become the green man; the power! Seriously, I know my siblings and I were not alone in squabbling over who would get to press the button, how our Mum

Figure 5.5 A 2-year-old girl child getting ready to cross the road safely.

decided each time I am not sure, but I am fairly sure the youngest got more turns than me. ...

Figure 5.5 shows an example of a road crossing that requires a button to be pressed to make something else happen which can be a daily occurrence for those of us who live in urban areas. Simply walking to nursery, to the shops, or to visit family will often require crossing a road and so a great learning opportunity. How does it work? What happens to the lights? Why does it make the sound? Noticing how the surface of the pavement at the crossing changes. All of these questions encourage conversation from a very simple button.

Push button feedback device

I have seen these appearing in a range of stores and entertainment venues such as cinemas and museums over the last two or three years. Usually a freestanding device with a few buttons. It asks "How was your visit?" and then encourages you to push the red, yellow, or green smiley face and give the venue instant feedback. A child can certainly do that and most of them can do it independently. On pressing the buttons, some light up, or flash, or even make a cheery noise to show thanks for pushing the button and providing feedback. Delightful.

Talking rubbish bins

Across the UK, there has been a drive to increase the number of public bins for our litter as well as for the things that can be recycled. Part of that drive has included providing some bins that give you feedback when you put your rubbish in. Once you have lifted the lid or pulled down the chute, you add your litter, and then get an audio response. It might be you a get a thank you or a chewing sound which I found amusing and I know children will love. So, the bins use technology to give that feedback, another example of cause and effect using sensors but also provides a chance to discuss good manners and the environmental impact of recycling.

Household and garden technology

This will be particularly relevant for those who work in home-based settings such as childminders and nannies but useful to consider for us all. In Figure 5.6, you can see a child helping to vacuum the carpet and a child is having a go at making apple juice using a traditional apple press.

Around the home there are lots of technology items and children helping to use them is a useful way for them to learn about the world around them.

The importance of real-world tech

Engaging with the technology that surrounds us isn't necessarily an obvious place for a child's learning but of course it can be. The objects that we interact with to access services and to make our lives easier are growing, and by acknowledging their presence and importance we open up the world a little bit more, for ourselves and for the children we work with. Some of the tech in the real world is there to make the world more accessible and as the world listens

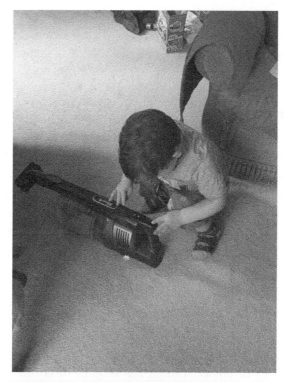

Figure 5.6 Photographs showing a 2-year-old helping with the vacuuming and a 3-year-old turning the handle of an apple press.

more and more to the disabled community, the technology will develop too. Of course, many of the tech used for access for those with disabilities actually make the world more accessible for us all.

The wider learning

Everything we experience as we grow and develop leads us to becoming the adult of the future, and as practitioners we should utilise each of those experiences to equip the children in our care to become the brilliant well-rounded individuals they each have the potential to be. Engaging in the real-world tech all around us is an important part of that. Children will gain much from the experiences explored in this chapter plus the many more you are able to offer as you explore the world together.

Children start to learn how to keep themselves safe and risk assess when they can cross the road safely, the road crossings are a key part of this. They gain independence from using the self-service machine in the library, or the push to open buttons on doors. They certainly will get a sense of achievement from many of the activities discussed and therefore gain in confidence. With growing confidence, they become more willing to try new things, to "have a go" and the skills in using one piece of equipment will gradually be transferred to other pieces of equipment, through trial and error they will discover more that they are able to do. Something else that children will develop through using technology is the ability to bounce back when things don't go to plan. In Chapter 7, I talk about some of the challenges with technology, and many of these are true whether you are three and using the tech for the first time, or an experienced adult. As adults, we can find it frustrating when the equipment doesn't do what we expected it to do, children will experience this too. We can all learn from taking a step back, maybe looking at the problem from a different angle and trying again. Turning it off and on again usually works best.

Everything in a child's world is an opportunity for learning to take place and a skilled adult noticing those opportunities can support them appropriately. Listening, observing, and waiting are crucial skills for the practitioner, it is all too easy to jump in and "solve" the problem for the child, or to "help" them figure it out, but often, if we wait, a child will find ways of working it out for themselves. This might include asking a trusted adult for help, so again we need to skilfully support, without taking over. I am always reminded of the title of that brilliant book by Julie Fisher, "Interacting not interfering" as a way to remind myself about what my role is in children's play. (The whole book is worth a read of course!)

Action list

Next time you take the children out for a walk in the local area, carry out a technology survey with the children (great maths links).

Make a list of all of the technology you encounter on a day out.

Reflective prompts – Technology beyond the setting

■ What skills do children need to engage with everyday technology? How can you encourage them to develop those skills?

Conclusion

Spend time noticing what is all around you; the technology you already engage with regularly (and not so regularly) and consider how these tools enhance, support, or challenge you. Then, find ways to incorporate those into your practice with children. Talk to colleagues about how they do this and challenge yourself to do this more. There is a world of possibilities for you and the children you work with and I hope you are able to see that and continue to use all that is available to create wonderful opportunities.

6 Technology for Staff
Making Your Role Easier

So far, this book has very much focused on how technology can be used with, for, and by children, how to engage them, support their learning and development, and capture their imagination as they learn about the world around them. This chapter moves the focus on to us, the practitioner and how technology can be harnessed to support our roles when we work with children. Many settings have turned to a range of technological solutions to aid their work, to streamline processes, and make communication with families more inclusive. We'll look at some of the solutions being used and examine them as well as consider how technology can support our development as professionals who strive to grow and improve our practice but are often time poor. I've decided to discuss the software options in a generic way rather than focusing on a specific company's software and I have not written it with the intention of convincing you to use it, simply to let you know what the options are and how to get the best of what they offer as well as considering what the pros and cons of using them are. I have tried to be balanced and do not endorse any of the technology mentioned which is for illustrative purposes only. It is important that before going ahead with a technology solution, you do your own research. Look at the software and compare what each package offers, consider the price and accessibility and I'd suggest reaching out to other settings and early years professionals and talk to them about what they use. Some of them will be discussed here and I hope they will give you food for thought.

DOI: 10.4324/9781003023173-7

Reducing paperwork?

When I started as a nursery nurse, we used a lot of paper. It was used to record observations, track development, monitor "stepping stones", send messages home and receive them back, record dietary requirements and share the menu with families and many more things besides. I am not saying that some of that is no longer necessary, but we should be more mindful in how much we use and how we can improve our environmental impact. Less paper is part of that process but it is important to remember that technology isn't in itself "green," it has its own environmental impact too. I also remember how I always felt I was not spending enough time with the children. Writing, recording, and monitoring always seemed to take time I wanted to be playing alongside the children. I know that some of the technology available now would certainly have given me some of that time back. Again, it is not a perfect solution but with practice it can take less time and make things more efficient.

An online recording system?

It is of course entirely possible that your setting has continued with the traditional methods of recording or you may have been using an online tool for years, something like Tapestry, Kinderley Together, Baby's Days, or Famly. It's also possible you are between the two and have no idea where to begin. I hope this will help.

Firstly, you don't have to use an online system, it may not be right for your families, setting and team and that is ok. However, if you do want to move to an online system then it is vital you do your research. Don't pick the cheapest, or the first one you hear about or the one the nursery down the road uses, take your time and explore the options. From my research, prices are broadly similar and are based on the size of your settings with some platforms being free for childminders and very small settings. Some have the option to add in functions such as payroll and other staffing processes. Some have integrated the new Development Matters, some Birth to 5 Matters and some have both. Some enable instant communication with families and some have more functions that you could ever need (just like most of our smartphones).

I've spoken to many practitioners over recent years and the biggest advantage to using an online system seems to be the time it saves, almost everyone says the process of tracking learning and development is quicker when using an online learning journal. I haven't carried out extensive research so this might be a perception, but I would argue that may be enough. If we feel like we have more time (even if we actually don't), could that make us more productive and effective in other areas of our work? The impact of feeling less time pressured surely would lead to us feeling more able to focus on the important aspects of the role, like relationship building and observing children.

The important skill of observation

I always say that I think the observation skills across the early years sector are second to none and that it takes dedication to do it so well. Observation is a skill and therefore something we can learn and improve with practice. Early years practitioners certainly get plenty of practice but writing in long hand is hard. Many of us struggle with the legibility of our writing when doing it quickly and I have known practitioners that have carried out an observation, and then written it out in neat, effectively doing it twice, that is a waste of time.

So, what solutions are there?

■ One is to use a coding system for observations to help speed up the writing, but of course, you have to learn the code and so does anyone who might be reading the observation such as parents.

■ Another is to talk through the observation and record it on a device. By speaking about what you see you may notice different things as your eyes are on the action at all times (instead of looking down at your paper). I wonder how disruptive this is for the children playing though, hearing a commentary of what they are doing interspersed with their name, that would be very distracting for me.

■ You can use a tablet to type your observation which avoids the handwriting issue but means you may be looking at your hands more, typing on a screen is not as easy as with a keyboard so may simply add to the challenges we already face as observers.

■ You could film the children and watch it back later as a way of being able to notice much more but again that will add to the time as you prepare the equipment, set the recording and then, give time to actually watching it back to ensure you are picking up the useful and noteworthy elements that can then feed into your tracking and planning.

Communication

Communication with parents and families is vital if we are to build and nurture relationships with them and work with them to provide the best care for their children. The ways in which we communicate needs to be as individual as each of the families we work with are. We know some of the parents respond best with face-to-face communication and where possible I advocate this as the first choice, but families have so many pulls on their time and attention that sometimes other methods will get the message through more clearly. Text messages using a range of different apps will work for some, whereas other parents will prefer an email. Some will like a phone call and others will interact freely via a social media platform. Some parents like to make an appointment, others prefer spontaneous connections. The key, of course, is to find out what works for each family and checking regularly that this is still the best way to connect (and that you have the most up-to-date contact information!). Technology can help with that too, think about how you record the preferred method of communication and ensure those who need to communicate know that.

Technology to support communication

Using technology is more than simply learning what it is does, in fact I think the most important element is confidence. The way to become more confident with technology is to use it, to practice and to try things out which in itself takes confidence. So, where do you start?

My top suggestion is to start simply and with something you already know or use in your own time. If you already use social media, is there a way of using this to communicate with parents safely? Your setting can create accounts and provide staff with access so you can communicate with families, without needing to use your personal account and therefore keeping you safe too.

Anything you use to communicate with family needs to be two way to ensure that you are building the relationship with them and they can reciprocate. Social media is one example, a private group, only open to those invited enables parents to share information and comments as well as the staff team.

Professionalism

Many times, I have heard a practitioner describe themselves as "just" an early year worker, "just" a childminder, "just" an assistant, I also hear people from outside of early years assume what we do is easy. Also, those in power rarely talk about our sector with the level of respect we see for other professions and yet, what we do in the early years literally helps set up a child for life. An enriching, impactful early years' experience can and does help children develop a love for learning, nurtures curiosity, and enables them to be themselves. That does not happen by luck, but by the dedication and hard work of every adult who works with them; you. To be seen as professionals, we must see ourselves as professionals, not "just" anything. Being a professional does not stop once we receive our certificate for an early years qualification but is something we strive to demonstrate throughout our careers. It is a state of being that requires work and effort on the part of the individual but also for those who work in settings the organisation we work with too. For childminders and other lone workers, it is important to build your own professional networks, and I know many of you do. Our connection with others supports our professional development and helps us raise our standards and strive for better.

Professional development is a cyclical process that is ongoing, it should be purposeful and meaningful and it should have impact. By cyclical I mean that it is always moving, and we review, plan, and do many times over our career, in smaller and larger cycles. By purposeful and meaningful, I am of course referring to the fact that whatever activities we participate in need to make sense, fit within a plan, be relevant to our role, our setting, and our practice. Finally, by having an impact, I mean it must do something. That might be shift our view, offer an alternative one, provide a new idea to try in practice, keep us informed of changes, help us reflect more effectively, or change something that is no longer working. The impact might be on us, our colleagues, our setting, or crucially on the children, and families that we serve (ideally, all of those!).

The multiple different ways we can engage in professional development will vary depending on such things as location, budget, and our own intrinsic motivation to want to do a better job. Some of these perceived barriers can be overcome by technology and because of the changes in the world following the COVID-19 outbreak, these approaches have been embraced more than ever.

Using technology to support professional development

So, if you are ready to learn about new approaches or emerging theories, to learn a new skill, start to see things from a new perspective, or to sharing new ideas, how might technology help that process?

With a quick search on the internet, you will find many online journals that are available for subscribing, many offer a free level of access with the option to pay and get full access. Nursery World is one such journal, it provides a practitioner with a source of up-to-date changes from the sector, news, and ideas as well as more in-depth articles that help you consider your practice and will start conversations amongst you and your colleagues.

Another great way to engage in the sector and keep up to date is to join online communities across a range of social media. Whichever platform you prefer, after a quick search you will find a plethora of spaces to learn, engage, share, and discuss all things early years. I'd recommend starting with KEYU (Keeping early years unique) for somewhere friendly, accurate, and non-judgemental.

Having said that, simply listening to others, reading, completing courses, observing others' practice, conversations, attending training, and conferences, taking part in practitioner research, active participation in EY communities, membership organisations, completing skills audit, and much more, all contribute to you and how you do your job.

How to find what works for you

Professional development comes in a wide range of experiences and from a wide range of people and sources, there is certainly no one size fits all here. So, if it so varied how do we know when we've found it and if it's right? When I am looking for ways to develop myself, I ask myself some questions.

■ Who is sharing their wisdom? Whether that is an opinion piece, a journal article, a training session, an online forum, who is sharing this information. What position are they sharing it from? Are they a practitioner, an "expert" a politician, or an academic? All can bring value but we need to clarify who is telling us this stuff, I also want to know their agenda. Are they trying to sell me something? Do they think their way is the only way? Have they researched it? Is it true and how do I know?

■ What information is being shared? A philosophy, an approach, a skill, an idea, top tips, legislation, policy update … Is that what I need?

■ Where – is the information accessible? Online or in person, behind a paywall, or openly accessible for all. Am I prepared to pay for this and if so, how much?

■ When – how much time do I need to give it and is it during work time? If it is in my free time, do I see enough value in it to give it that time?

- Why – what drew me to it, does it help me fill a gap in my knowledge or skill set? Does it challenge my thinking? Does it build on something I already know about; does it provide a new perspective?

- How – a one off webinar? A series of articles in a monthly journal, four years of study, a short documentary ....

Reflective practice

Alongside my passion for technology is my passion for reflective practice and professional development. The huge importance for each of us as professional early years practitioners to continuously develop what we do and how we do it so that we increase the impact we have on the lives of the children that we work with, and their families is not to be underestimated.

What is reflective practice?

Listening, noticing, observing what we do, analysing what we do well, what we can learn from, identifying missed opportunities, acknowledging our strengths, learning from errors and mistakes, being aware of our weaknesses, working towards developing those weaknesses, challenging ourselves, challenging others, being honest with ourselves and others, considering what next? Thinking so what? Pondering on progress

Reflective practice and professional development

Part of our professional development should also include us as a reflective practitioner. Without reflection are we really aware of what we need, of what will support our development and how that fits with our role and setting?

Being a reflective practitioner is about looking back and forward, it requires honesty and accepting constructive criticism.

How to be reflective

Reflection can be done in a range of ways and again the key is to find the way that works best for you, as long it supports you to notice what you do well and where you can improve, it works.

Some of us choose to write this down, using a simple notebook or a word document on the computer. Some of us like a blank page and some of us prefer a structure.

Many of us are aware of the simple and very effective approach to reflection, plan, do, and review and we use it when we work with children to help us identify what has worked with particular resources or experiences we offer. It is important to apply it to our practice too. We might be comfortable with this approach but there are others to try and that may give you a more in-depth view of your practice and lead to deeper understanding of what you are and why.

You may have come across a tool known as SWOT analysis. SWOT stands for strengths, weaknesses, opportunities, and threats. It is possible to carry out a SWOT analysis on yourself but my experience of these tells me they work really well when we look at them as a team and see what each of the members bring to the effectiveness of how you work, you also identify any gaps and this can be useful when looking to recruit new team members. This can be done without any technology at all, simply using pens and paper, but you could co-create it online using a tool such as Mural (https://www.mural.co/) or Google Jamboard (https://edu.google.com/intl/ALL_uk/jamboard/) where contributors can be anonymous and might be more honest. This will open up the conversation and could lead to more honest conversations about how each team member contributes and what more they can do.

Similarly, you might find carrying out a skills audit can be helpful and might lead to similarly powerful conversations. This again can be done on paper, but there are online tools which can support the analysis of the results which could add value to the process. What skills do you feel are needed to do your role, or the one you plan to apply for need? Then you decide which ones you have or not and to what extent, often skills audits use a scoring system. This can be useful when done across a team especially if there is a need to recruit new staff.

My favourite structured approach to reflection is to use the reflective lenses model created by S Brookfield (1995). It provides structure as well as real depth to my reflection whist considering my practice from a range of perspectives, or lenses. Again, this can be done simply on paper or online and can be done alone or with colleagues for team reflection.

Future me (https://www.futureme.org/) is a website I came across recently that can be used as some accountability for any actions you set yourself. You can write yourself a letter using the site and in six months/a year's time it will email you so you can review your progress.

Setting habits for reflection is important and like any habit, can be formed starting now. However, before you settle on your own reflection habits, I encourage you to experiment first and find what works and doesn't, for you; some reflection on reflective practice if you will.

One really important aspect of reflective practice is that you should have control over it, it is for and by you, of course whatever you engage with will impact your role within a team and setting but that should not be the primary focus. If you take responsibility for your own development, you are more likely to engage with the learning you need, trust yourself the way we trust children to know what play they require to develop. You will be and feel more empowered and more likely to see reflection as an ongoing process with real value.

A note to managers, aside from the statutory training such as safeguarding, it really benefits the organisation if individuals are fully engaged with and in control of their own development and it takes the pressure off of you. Plan development together with the team and watch them grow.

Reflective prompts – Technology for staff

- Do you use technology in your role? What equipment and in what ways?

- Does it support your role or add barriers? In what ways?

- How can these barriers be overcome?

- What areas of your role are most challenging? Could technology help manage these challenges?

Conclusion

Continually wanting to do the best for the families we serve is a key driver for those who work professionally with children, going above and beyond is standard for many of us and feeling like there are not enough hours in the day is shared across the sector. We are all trying to fit more in and being creative with how we can support, how we can develop ourselves, how we keep up with the ever-changing demands of the role is crucial if we are to feel that sense of pride and satisfaction that comes with doing a good job. Technology can provide some of those creative solutions, but I recognise they do not create more time or solve everything. I do encourage you to try out something new, to be brave and embrace a new way of doing things. Whether that is something to support communication with families, a new way of reflecting on your practice or engaging in some online development opportunities, just give it a go.

7 Pause for Thought
Barriers to Using Technology

Often the first thing I hear when I mention using technology with young children is a concern for their welfare and obviously, that should always be a top consideration whatever we are planning to do with children. This shouldn't, however, be seen as a reason to not use technology at all. Keeping children safe is crucial but so is offering a range of learning opportunities and experiences, it is hard to do that if we miss out a large area because we worry about the safety alone. Risk assessment is a powerful tool to ensure the environment, the people, and the resources are as *safe as necessary* to ensure the children have freedom and opportunities to explore and express themselves.

This chapter acknowledges the potential hazards and concerns of using technology with young children and will explore ways that these can be overcome if we are willing to try. It tackles the safeguarding concerns practitioners have and then discusses ways to teach children about keeping themselves safe. The chapter ends with a discussion around the importance of having an open culture in which children and adults feel safe to explore and share their own concerns.

Challenge number 1 – The technology can go wrong

Yes, I know it's not meant to, but it can and does. It is possible that the technology will not work, not do what you expect, keep intermittently beeping for no obvious reason, or just stop part way through use. This puts some of us off using it at all and is a convenient excuse, who needs the hassle; we've got enough to be doing already. To overcome this mindset, it is important that we develop our levels of "tech tolerance" and support those around us to develop it too. Tech tolerance is accepting that the

DOI: 10.4324/9781003023173-8

technology will not always work, that some users may struggle with it and not understand how to use elements of it and being able to deal with that without the desire to simply throw it out of the nearest window. It calls upon our resilience and restraint as well as our problem solving and patience, things I know early years practitioners have in abundance. How do we help those around us to develop the levels of tech tolerance required though? The most important thing is to model it. When things go wrong, show your own tech tolerance with confidence, children will respond accordingly, as will colleagues. Show not tell is a tried and tested way of teaching others which you well know, so more of that please.

Challenge number 2 – The technology is dead

Some technology will need batteries and some need charging. Both of these require an adult to have stocked spare batteries or remembered to plug in the device before the end of the day, so it is ready for the next session. Therefore, adding another task for already overstretched staff. It is important though that when a child shows interest in a piece of equipment it can be used in the moment so we really can follow their interest and show we are listening to them and their needs. That is not to say that there isn't learning to come out of a time when they want to explore something, but it doesn't work – there's a real opportunity for quality interactions. "I wonder what's wrong?" "How did that happen?" "How can we make it work?" wonderful open questions to develop sustained shared thinking with children and provide a model of tech tolerance. You can also encourage the children to take control of the process of charging devices when they have finished using it. Some will have a docking or charging station, so the child simply needs to put it back which avoids them having to actually plug in the device, really simple.

Challenge number 3 – Children disengage with the world around them

It is true that some technology toys and resources designed for children do not promote working with others and specifically require just one person to control or use them. This can and will lead to some users becoming so absorbed in the task that they zone out from their surroundings and become completely submerged in the technology. I would argue this is a character-istic we are hoping children will develop. "Maintain focus on their activity for a period of time," and "not easily distracted" are a feature of the active learning characteristic of effective learning. We want children to be able to keep focus and if we observed this in the water tray, where a 3-year-old might spend seven or eight minutes absorbed in pouring water through a water wheel, over and over again, we would record this and talk to them about their activity. What is the difference? A water wheel is a great piece of technology too.

Challenge number 4 – The socio-economic impact (disparity)

Some practitioners worry that using technology in settings shows children what they are missing at home or, if they have good access to technology at home that they simply do not need access to it whilst in the setting. They feel it flashes a spotlight on the differences in home life that seems unfair and might cause upset.

If there is a symbol that represents quite how divided society is, I agree tech-nology is it. In 2019, 79% of adults in the UK owned a smartphone and the percentage of households with internet access was 87% (https://www.ofcom.org.uk/__data/assets/pdf_file/0028/155278/communications-market-report-2019.pdf).

We can assume then the large majority of children have access to the internet. But what of the 13% of households that do not have access? There will of course be a number of households who actively choose not to have internet access but that leaves a % of households who simply cannot afford to connect to the internet or the access in their geographical area is poor. According to the ONS in 2019 of the 13% who did not have internet access in the home, 30% stated the cost as a factor. A large number of those house-holds will be living without an income that meets the minimum living standards and will include children (https://commonslibrary.parliament.uk/research-briefings/sn07096/).

So, are we highlighting inequality if we promote the use of technology in our settings or helping to redress the balance? I would argue that we are redressing the balance by including a rich range of resources and this directly links to the cultural capital agenda as well as the school readiness one. We build on what children already know to learn about the world around them, but we must also introduce them to things they have no experience of too; tech could and should be one of those things.

Challenge number 5 – Fine motor skills can be neglected

The worry that technology might lead to a lack of development, different skills being developed or some skills being left behind.

I remember back in 2012 or 2013 there was real concern about young children picking up books and being frustrated that "swiping" did not turn pages, (and plenty since too). Adults, those working in Early Years and plenty not, had a lot to say about it too. People seemed very unhappy and concerned that children would lose the use of their fingers for things like page turning. As adults, we have learnt a whole range of new skills but retain the older ones and children are much more ready for new learning than us as we age.

So, is this the reality? Are children not able to distinguish between a screen and a book? Have children stopped being able to turn pages if they spend "all" their time on a tablet?

I am sure initially, if they have only encountered one or the other, this might happen, but children adapt quickly. They can do both, just as we can. I also don't think children are spending all of their time on a tablet and I'm not advocating they do either. Technology is much wider than "just" computers and many of the resources you have access to, and I talk about in this book will provide opportunities to use fine motor skills in a range of ways.

Challenge number 6 – Gross motor skills not being targeted, the misconception that using technology is sedentary

Another big concern around the use of technology is that children do not move around. Certainly, if we talk about technology to mean only computers that are plugged in to a socket, they will not move around very much at all, but technology is such a broad term that lots of pieces of technology equipment provide an opportunity to move. Take one example of a camera: children will rarely sit in one spot to take photos; they will travel quite a large distance around the setting capturing their viewpoint to share with their friends. If we are using the narrow view of technology to mean computers then we can make it more active by removing chairs for example, have a stand-up computer desk, or tablets instead of a laptop/desktop so it can travel around the setting. Certainly, rules around time-limits will be essential too. It is not good for any of us to sit for too long at a screen. Regular breaks from the same activity is good practice. The World Health Organisation (WHO, 2019) recommends that under ones have no sedentary screen time and those children aged 2, 3 and 4 years should have no longer than one hour of sedentary screen time in any one day, not all in one go.

Challenge number 7 – Eye problems

"If you watch too much TV your eyes will go square," I heard that a fair amount when I was a child and I guess lots of you did too, you might even have said it to your own children. It is not true (in case you were not sure) but there are some links to overuse of screens and problems with your eyes almost all of the research into this is about teenagers and adults not young children making it very difficult to make good, informed decisions. It is possible to alleviate problems though such as not sitting too closely to screens, turning down brightness and colour contrasts and having eye breaks regularly. The RNIB recommends the 20:20:20 rule for older children and adults; look away from the screen every 20 minutes, for 20 seconds, focusing on something 20 feet away. For children I would suggest they are not using the screen for longer than 10 minutes at a time, and during that time should look away from the screen frequently. This is easily achieved if the screen time is being shared with an adult who can reinforce this, encourage this, model this for the child, and build in those healthy habits.

Challenge number 8 – Attention/Concentration

It has been suggested that children using technology and, in particular, screens struggle with concentration and maintaining attention on non technological activities, there is some research to support this that found long-term television viewing at ages 1–3 years old predicts attention and hyperactivity difficulties among 7 year olds. (PHE 2013). The suggestions and recommendations made above relating to eye problems should be applied here too, along with a healthy dose of common sense. Everything or anything in moderation.

Challenge number 9 – Missing out on other things

If the technology is good, even too good, children will not want to play with anything else.

As with anything, variety is the spice of life. Children need a range of experiences and as adults you can set boundaries and rules to support this. It is good practice to have maximum times for screen use as stated above. The limits recommended by WHO are across the whole day, so if children have had 30 minutes with you in the setting, their parents should limit the screen time at home to no more than an additional 30 minutes. Again though, this isn't just about screens, so setting time limits for other technology is useful not least in terms of access, it means more children will be able to "have a go" if they want to at the same time as learning about turn-taking.

Staff need to model time limits on their use of such things as cameras and tablets in the setting and to inform parents and carers about time limits at home too, sharing what access children have had in the setting and reinforcing positive habit messages about reduced time for all of us.

Challenge number 10 – Impact on sleep

Too much screen time, especially close to bedtime can impact on the quality of sleep and as children seem to be getting less sleep than they need we need to promote good sleep hygiene to families that includes no screens for at least 1 hour before bedtime. As well as enough physical activity during the day and reduced screen time overall along with a good restful routine at bedtimes will encourage this.

Challenge number 11 – Safeguarding concerns of using web-enabled devices such as computers, tablets, phones, and smart speakers

In recent years, we have become more aware of the potential dangers of being online and if you are a child or young adult, the risks seem far greater. In a white paper published in 2019 by the UK government, it stated that in 2018 in the UK there had been a 50% increase in child sexual abuse material reported and Facebook had removed 8.7 billion pieces of content globally that breached their rules about child nudity and exploitation. That is a staggering number and rightly causes people to feel anxious about allowing children to go online. I am not going to pretend that is not scary, it is, but it is possible to use the internet and protect yourself and your children from such content for the majority of time you access it. It is also important to teach children how to keep themselves safe online and what to do if they feel unsafe, if someone they do not know messages them and to talk about their use so it is not secretive and therefore something that can be hidden from adults.

It is important to state that all social media platforms have a minimum age limit so the children in our settings should not have accounts or access to accounts of others, that doesn't mean that they don't have access though. In fact, as mentioned in Chapter 2, the most recent Ofcom "Children and Parents Media Use and Attitudes Report" (2018 – released in January 2019) found that: 1% of 3- to 4-year-olds have their own smartphone and 19% have their own tablet 52% of 3- to 4-year olds go online for an average of nearly nine hours a week 45% of 3- to 4-year-olds use YouTube.

All settings have a safeguarding policy. In recent years, we have updated them to include such things as staff not taking their own devices into the rooms. It is also important to have a policy (or include a statement in your safeguarding policy) about how to safely use the internet-enabled devices that are supplied for staff and children. This will include how staff should talk about it with children, how to enable children to keep themselves safe online, software used, and appropriate use and sharing information with parents and carers safely.

We know the internet is a wonderful resource and has unlimited amounts of learning potential for us and the children we work with, we know there is more content to entertain than any of us will ever get to the end of and more cat videos than any of us will ever need. We are also well aware of the potential dangers that lurk within the web. The inappropriate content, the offensive comments, the images that we can never unsee, and the people that are behind that content that are intent on causing harm (and making money).

So, as an early years practitioner how do we balance that to make the most of the opportunities whilst also mitigating the risks and keeping the children safe?

A clear policy with boundaries, good role modelling, and sharing our learning with children, families and each other are good places to start. I've included a sample policy later in this chapter which you can use to create or update your own and thoughts about the open culture I think is required to keep us all safe in the online world.

Giving children skills to keep themselves safe online

One of the most important things about supporting children to use technology and in particular the internet is to teach them the skills to keep themselves safe whilst using these tools.

There will be many times, many hours, when a child is able to access these resources and the internet without a safe adult around to really observe what is happening and use the internet alongside the child.

I think of it as similar to when we teach children about crossing the road safely. Initially an adult will hold the child's hand and tell them when it safe to cross, but, ultimately, we have to teach children to look and listen for themselves and make their decision about when it is safe, they have to judge the risks and manage them alone.

So, how do we teach children about being safe online and when does it begin? As with almost anything, it starts as soon as they are observing those around them using technology. We are role modelling all of the time, they notice everything we do and our behaviour with technology is no different. With that in mind I suggest noticing how you and your colleagues use technology and the behaviours you model to the children. Peer observation is a powerful tool and we all learn from it. Raise this as a suggestion in your next team meeting, if you already use peer observation, suggest you look at technology behaviours, and if you don't yet use it, this is a gentle way to introduce it.

If you use tablets for recording observations and development, they are likely to be around the setting a lot and so it can be useful to observe how they are used. You could do a simple event sample to record how often each member of staff picks up the tablet and uses it. You could do a narrative observation and write down the behaviours you see. You could create a checklist and tick off the behaviours you spot. You could also do this for other equipment such as cameras and desk top computers/laptops that are available for use by the children and spend time noticing the way the adult models directly for the child.

An example of an observation checklist for technology behaviours

Practitioner:
Date:

Behaviour description	Seen Y/N	Comments
Only touch or pick up the tablet when using it for work (not walking around with it)		
Returning tablet to the agreed point after each use (e.g. on charge)		
Remaining aware of surroundings whilst using the tablet		
Engaging in conversation with children when approached – stopping and looking at the child		
Answering questions about what you are doing online		
Showing the interested child what you are doing on the tablet		
When appropriate, allowing the child to take charge of the tablet		

Things to consider when observing

■ Do adults only use the device when necessary or when a child initiates it?

■ Do adults encourage the child to control the device for themselves?

■ Does the adult talk about safety in any sense whilst using the device with a child? For example, reinforcing the importance of doing this alongside an adult, or checking you are clicking on or selecting what you intended to.

■ When the adult is in control of the device, do they give the child/ren a commentary about how they are accessing different elements?

■ During the activity does the adult provide positive comments to reinforce good habits being formed/used?

Once you have carried out some peer observations of the staff behaviour around technology, take some time to discuss what it tells you and consider ways you can improve your practice in this area. You don't have to try and get things perfect, take 1 action and ensure this is implemented fully and then move on to another. That way good habits will be formed and you'll all feel more confident in those things. You can also agree how you will each support each other.

Smart speakers are a fairly recent addition to the early years space and provide opportunities to access the internet even before you can read and write. Simply being able to ask a question or give a command can be a more inclusive way to include technology into your practice. It goes without saying though that we still need to consider how we keep children safe when using one. Expectations about usage are important, for example, an agreement that if the smart speaker is playing music, you should wait until it is finished before asking something else of it. Or, check with an adult first. Ensuring the usual parental locks are in place for what can be accessed is important and all of the current smart speakers have these options.

Another key time that children learn about being safe online is when they begin to use the tools or going online for the first time themselves. It is important that access to technology especially that which is internet enabled is supervised by safe adults, at home this may not always happen, but in our settings, we can ensure it does. As with anything we do 1:1 with children, it enables us to further build on relationships and teach them not just about the technology. Encouraging children to talk about what they are doing online and what they are learning about is important, no matter their age. It is also important to encourage them to say when they are unsure or need help. Modelling this is important but also responding positively when they do this (as in any other activity where this is common practice).

There are online safety rules that are useful to adopt in your setting and these talk about the importance of equipping children. For example, as they get older, do they know how to report content that makes them feel worried? Do they have a safe adult they can talk to in a non-judgmental way about what they've been doing online? It can be harder to find advice for those of us who work with under 5s but there is guidance available such as that from Childnet and internet matters.

It is advisable to encourage parents to adopt the same rules at home too. Many adults feel ill-equipped to keep children safe online so sharing what you do as a setting is a way of supporting them. There are other ways you can involve the families you work with such as sharing some of the resources you use, including top tips in your newsletters and across your social media and website. At your next event for parents (stay and play/parents evenings/welcome events) you could display information for them to look while they wait. If you have a notice board in the entrance area, could you have a display there? Maybe if you are feeling very confident you could host an information session which of could be online or in person, where you talk about how you work towards keeping everyone safe online and what families can do at home to do the same. Your local early years team will have information and may have an advisor who specialises in this area, you could invite them along too.

Time and again I see and hear that parents and practitioners don't know what the children are doing online and for that reason alone, creating a culture of openness and mutual respect is vital if we are to keep children safe online. Allowing children to share what they are doing online without fear of judgement or criticism from the adults around them will help them feel they can be honest and ask questions as well as come to you when they feel unsafe or unsure of things they discover online.

Reflective prompt – Pause for thought

- What concerns you most about using technology with children? Why do you hold those concerns? What has influenced them?

- How can you ensure children are safe online?

I believe that when used purposefully, technology can only enhance a child's learning. Make sure you use a robust risk assessment process and talk openly to the team about their concerns that way, you will come up with practical solutions and learn together about the benefits to the children as well as to us, the practitioner.

Conclusion

Despite being a self-proclaimed technology enthusiast, I am fully aware of the challenges that many face when using it as well as some of the perceptions and nervousness around using with children. So this chapter has been written in an attempt to address many of these concerns by offering solutions. Many of them can be overcome with preparation, patience, and practice along with the desire to find the best ways of supporting children to learn.

I've given you a range of practical ways to manage the challenges as they occur as well as some strategies to prevent them such as teaching children how to be safe with the equipment alongside a short observation template and below you will find a sample policy to support your practice which I hope you will find useful and reassuring.

There's also a wealth of information out there and so to help you on your search for good information I've also ended the chapter with a list of helpful resources.

A sample policy

feel free to take the bits that fit your own circumstances and reword to suit your setting.

All staff must read the policy and sign to say they understand it and will adhere to it at all times.

All staff must attend a staff briefing about using online devices in the setting.

All staff are expected to attend an introductory training such as the e-learning on www.thinkuknow.co.uk. The DSL will attend an appropriate training delivered by the local safeguarding board.

Staff are issued with a Wi-Fi-enabled tablet for work purposes only. The device can be used during work hours and must be locked away in the office when not in use and overnight.

Before the tablet is issued to staff it will have safety software installed such as controls and blocks on certain websites. The devices issued for use by and with children will have the same set up.

All apps required for your role will be added to the device along with some apps considered suitable for children to access.

The camera and video will auto save to the setting's cloud storage only and this can only be used to send photos and videos to families using the online system used.

Any photos and videos stored in the cloud system can be used for work relating to the setting such as on its website.

The devices provided for children will be pre-loaded with suitable apps and these will be reviewed regularly.

Children can use the device on request but must be supervised at all times; ideally you will use the device alongside each other and ensure you talk about the processes as well as the game or website being accessed. Their time on a device should be limited to 10 minutes at any one time.

Staff should restrict their own use of tablets for the purpose of observation and tracking to the minimum so that they maximise their time with the children and model safe use.

The device should be stored away from children when not being used by staff for observation and tracking or when working with a child to ensure it is safe.

Staff should openly talk about their use of the devices and share what they do with children and be ready to respond to questions openly and honestly.

The tablets are not to be used for any personal activities except in the circumstance that it has been agreed the device can be loaned to the staff members for the duration of a course.

If inappropriate content is inadvertently accessed and or viewed by staff or children, the device must be turned off immediately and returned to the office. It must be reported to the designated safeguarding lead (DSL) and logged in the incident book. The DSL will advise on any next steps required.

Resources

https://www.ofcom.org.uk/__data/assets/pdf_file/0024/234609/childrens-media-use-and-attitudes-report-2022.pdf

https://www.ofcom.org.uk/research-and-data/multi-sector-research/cmr/cmr-2019

https://commonslibrary.parliament.uk/research-briefings/sn07096/

https://www.ons.gov.uk/peoplepopulationandcommunity/householdcharacteristics/homeinternetandsocialmediausage/bulletins/internetaccesshouseholdsandindividuals/2019

https://assets.publishing.service.gov.uk/government/uploads/system/uploads/attachment_data/file/793360/Online_Harms_White_Paper.pdf

https://www.gov.uk/government/publications/digital-resilience-framework, Digital resilience framework

https://www.drwg.org.uk/, Digital resilience working group

https://www.gov.uk/government/publications/safeguarding-children-and-protecting-professionals-in-early-years-settings-online-safety-considerations, UK Government online safety guidance for practitioners and managers

thinkuknow, https://www.thinkuknow.co.uk/professionals/resources/

internet matters, https://www.internetmatters.org/advice/0-5/

NSPCC, https://learning.nspcc.org.uk/

8 What Next?

In this final chapter, I talk about Tech champions, what that means, who can become one, and what they can do to develop the technology use in your setting. I've also included some helpful resources to support this. I then discuss microlearning and how this can enhance the CPD around technology in your setting and put the practitioner at the heart of the process.

I end the chapter by talking about the global situation surrounding the recent coronavirus pandemic (which is of course ongoing and leaving a lasting effect) and how technology has helped us and can continue to do so.

Tech champions and where to find them

When we describe someone as a champion of a principle or cause, we think of them as the person who will raise the status and visibility of that idea. Someone who keeps that idea at the front of our minds and ensures it is not missed during discussion and actions relating to other issues. Someone who will speak up for it positively when others may be dissenting, being reluctant to try something new or are closed off to the idea that is being proposed. A champion will be someone who can find the benefits and encourage others to see them too.

With anything that is new or that requires a focus it can be helpful to assign some responsibility to a team member. This can be anyone, but it should be someone that cares about technology (not just the youngest member of the team, the latest person to join the setting or someone who doesn't yet have an extra responsibility.)

DOI: 10.4324/9781003023173-9

Below I've provided a person specification which might help you think about who could be a tech champion for your setting.

First, let's look at how we might find a staff tech champion

I always prefer to find volunteers to take on additional responsibilities, someone who willingly offers to take something on in general is more likely to see it through.

They are more likely to bring their own ideas to the task and be enthusiastic about the topic. They can see why it's important to champion this particular thing and may already have some knowledge and skills in the area, although that is not necessary.

I also find personal and direct requests work most effectively rather than general, does anyone want to do this?' type requests. So, who in your setting might like the challenge of being a tech champion? Who would like to be asked to share their enthusiasm, their skills, their ideas with the rest of the team? You may find several people spring to mind, just one or maybe, it's not that easy and no one instantly pops up.

You could raise the idea at a team meeting and notice who responds positively to the discussion.

We want to support our children to be more tech savvy and want your ideas of how we do this

Opening the discussion in this way allows all ideas to be shared and can lead to you finding someone who could become a champion, you might even get someone to offer their time to this.

You could create an advert for the team board or staff room, or if you have a shared online space for the staff, add something in there.

I'd also advocate a role-share. Having people work together on projects is a great way of sharing the load but it also helps people to be accountable for the project and to their partner.

Once you have found one or two tech champions, ensure you talk together to agree the scope of the role, what the expectations are, how you will review the progress. For example, how much time would you expect them to spend on this project? Is there any budget? Can they have a slot in the team meetings to share ideas and encourage others to get involved? Is there training they can attend? What other resources might be available to them? How often will you review what is happening and how will you know their role is effective? How are you measuring the impact?

As with any initiative, it is important to see the impact it has so agreeing what success looks like helps to focus on how to get there. I'd certainly look for measures that are already present such as child observations, and other records already kept. This should not be an exercise in adding more paperwork to the team. Does tech feature in children's play more? Are parents and carers asking questions about how to keep their child safe online and did they attend the drop-in session you held to discuss how to do this. I've included an example agreement that you can adapt and use to suit your own settings plans.

A young tech champion?

So, we've got staff on board, can we also include the children in the plan? Well, of course, what is the early years without the children? Let's talk about encouraging children to be a tech champion.

Once again, we need willing volunteers and once again we need to set expectations about what this might involve. We also need to think about how we review progress, we all know that children love being given responsibilities and tasks to help, and this is one of the many roles they can really get stuck into. I suspect, if you find the right volunteers you'll get some brilliant ideas too about how to get everyone to be more tech aware.

Once again, I've included a sample person specification for a child tech champion but what else do we need to think about?

Firstly, we need to think about age-appropriateness as I am not suggesting our youngest children are tasked with such responsibility, but certainly from around three children could absolutely be involved in supporting the settings tech agenda.

Your observations are key here, you may already have noticed which children are more confident with the various tech resources you already have available in the setting and therefore, you might decide to follow the interests of that child to talk to them directly about the idea of being a tech champion.

Simply providing access to the resources and watching who interacts and how will give you insights and spark conversations to explore what they know and how they feel about using technology. Of course, it is likely the child will see it as just another resource, children tend not to put things in boxes the way adults do, that in itself is a useful attribute for a tech champion.

Circle time provides an opportunity for children to share what they know about technology, what resources they use and how they use them. It can prompt conversations about how they keep themselves safe too. You can also use circle time to discuss how we can each help around the setting, special jobs we can all do and responsibility.

The use of stories, puppets, props, and songs is not new to us and these can be used to great effect to open up discussions. This could then lead to choosing a tech champion or two. This could be rotated to give everyone who wants one a turn, as often happens with "jobs for children."

I've suggested agreeing with tech champions what the role looks like and for the children, I would advocate doing this with a group of children or even as appropriate, all of them.

Person specification – Tech champion (staff)

	Essential	**Desirable**
Knowledge	Child development Safeguarding What counts as technology	Variety of tech tools/resources
Skills	Turn things off and on Critical thinking Research Reflective Ability to demonstrate tools at variety of levels Problem-solving	Making complex ideas simple Speaking out at meetings
Attributes	Open-minded Resourceful Adaptable Patient Commitment	

Experience	Things like using a smart phone,
	  Digital TV, Microwave, Camera,
	  online shopping
		Video calls (zoom), sharing
		  resources online,

Qualifications	None	Early Years qual

Attitude	Willingness to share best practice
	Positive approach to how tech can
	  enhance children's lives, futures and
	  those of the adults around them
	Openness to CPD	

Person specification – Tech champion (child)

	Essential	Desirable
Knowledge	Turning things on/off Good control and co-ordination in small movements Can handle equipment and tools effectively	
Skills	Play, communication	
Attributes	Enjoys using tech in play	
Experience	Being a child	
Attitude	Curious, kind, loves to share	

Create an agreement

Along with a person specification to help identify who might be your tech champions, it is useful to have an informal agreement about what they will do in the role, what the expectations are and how you'll know the role is having an impact.

To do this, I would always encourage a collaborative approach, do it with the tech champion, and perhaps the rest of the team and children. What do we all need from the role and what will support us all to be engaged with the tech? Next in this chapter I talk about microlearning, this could be a useful tool for developing the agreement in a team meeting. For children, it might be a small circle time, or using a story to explore the idea of helping others to think about what works.

Whatever you do, the following questions might help to shape the conversation and lead to an agreement that the tech champions have ownership of; this means they are more likely to deliver.

Example questions to create an agreement for the staff tech champion project

- ■ What is the aim of the project?
- ■ What are the outcomes we want to see?
- ■ How will we measure those outcomes?
- ■ How often will we review the role?
- ■ What actions will we take to meet those outcomes?
- ■ What resources and support need to be in place?

Example questions to create an agreement for the child tech champion

How can you help your friends to use the resources? (Insert specific resources here)

How will we know if your help has worked?

What help do you need from the adults to be our tech champion?

Microlearning

Microlearning typically refers to learning in small chunks of time or learning small blocks of information. It is really useful for any professional wanting to develop but find themselves time poor as well as those who then also have wide ranging responsibilities and interests away from work (most of us).

Having just one objective or intended outcome helps to keep things focussed and can simplify the activity. For example, starting with an outcome of having a shared understanding of technology for the team can be met by asking "what does technology mean for us?" You could start by creating a word cloud together (using a tool like Mentimeter), this could be used to lead a discussion, and then together you can create a shared statement that the whole team has ownership of that clearly answers the question.

Microlearning is a useful method of accessing CPD and very quickly can add up to hours over a term or year barely without us noticing. More importantly, it can shift our practice in more direct and impactful ways when we are not overloading our brains with significant amounts of information that "gets" in the way of the learning. Being able to focus on just one element that we want to engage with instead of needing to filter through the less useful parts allows our brain to take on the information and process it, assimilating it to what we already know and think about how we can apply this to our work.

The concept of microlearning comes from the world of technology so it is entirely appropriate I should mention it here in this book, it's also possible you are already using this approach in some of your professional development and maybe you haven't realised it. Perhaps you have some examples of how you a have used this and could share those ideas with your team?

You can use a range of resources and methods for microlearning, and anyone can take a lead in the 'teaching' including you, this means it is a very democratic way of learning and sharing learning and is more inclusive than some more traditional approaches to development.

Examples of microlearning that link to use of technology in early years

Define technology in relation to early years – this could start with creating a word cloud and then lead into a discussion where you agree on what technology means to your setting and team.

Watch a video clip (such as those on the literacy trust website https://literacytrust.org.uk/resources/digital-technology-and-early-years/) and notice how the children respond to the technology and what they learn

Colleagues can take turns in showcasing a piece of technology in a team meeting – demonstration e.g. Bee-Bots, a new camera, walkie-talkies, and so on.

Read a short article and talk to the person next to you – what did you learn? Share the key points and then consider how these could support the development of your own setting, or not.

Carry out a technology audit, list what equipment you have, check it works, then as a team consider how you can use each item. You could then do a list of all the benefits of using each piece of equipment within the setting to make informed decisions.

Explore this article and video (https://sites.google.com/sheffield.ac.uk/makey/resources/for-educators/case-studies-schools/Monteney-Nursery?authuser=0), discuss what you notice and what you can take away to inform your own practice.

The key to any professional development activity is the impact it has on the learner and their practice. If you attend a workshop, watch a documentary, read an article, or observe a colleague and all that happens is you tick it off of a list, mostly, you may as well not have bothered. If, however, you attend a workshop and something is shared that makes you stop, reflect, think, and plan, that was worth the other 2 hours and 55 minutes you attended. So, how do we know if the professional development activities we engage in do have an impact? One way is through our reflective practice, and I talked about this in Chapter 6. Looking back to see how far we've come with our thinking and development is crucial. Another way I know if something I've learnt has impact is if I want to talk about it and share it with others. I don't just mean a quick hit of the share button on social media, but having conversations with people, sending them the direct link via email with a why you should watch this comment or sending a copy of the article in the post (how novel!). Often, when I share it, I find it helps to clarify my thinking about the point further and can spark other ways I can implement the learning; it's an exciting part of the process.

You will find professional development opportunities everywhere and online is a good place to start. Some of the opportunities will be aimed at practitioners with little experience at the start of their early years journey and some for those with more experience. Some will be standalone short courses.

Tech in a post-COVID world

Since the outbreak of Coronavirus, we have seen a massive shift to a wider reliance on technology to keep us connected. There can't be a sector that hasn't needed to embrace more technology to enable them to keep going and early years is no exception.

Immediately, staff across the sector looked for and found ways to adapt to the situation and ensure they continued to provide a high level of service to their families.

A global pandemic

At the start of 2020, the world had to adapt to respond to the global pandemic caused by coronavirus, for large parts of the world, this involved full national lockdowns and in March 2020, the UK did just that. Lots of industries shut down or reduced operations to the bare minimum, those who could were ordered to "work from home" and public transport stopped.

The early years sector was to remain open as an essential service providing childcare for parents who were required to attend a workplace such as healthcare settings and education. They were also asked to remain open to provide vital support for those children with additional needs and who would therefore potentially have the greatest impact of not attending. For some early settings this meant they were at near or full capacity, and things simply carried on "as usual." Only now, families and staff were concerned about the virus and things did change. Everyone was much more aware of hand hygiene, people weren't in the usual groupings or rooms, perhaps staff had to work with different children and parents were unable to enter the settings to drop off and collect their children. Some families kept their children home, some staff needed to remain home to protect their own families, and of course, a lot of people got sick and simply couldn't work. So, the sector couldn't carry on as "normal." The sector had to adapt and find new ways of working, they had to be even more flexible in their approach and my goodness did they.

Home-learning

For children not coming to the setting there was a need for activities, things to do and families were in need of support to keep their children learning. Home-learning was the response, and this took many forms. The professionals that make up the early years sector got creative. Some of you created home-learning packs consisting of activity ideas, some of you sent links to great websites for families to access, or apps to download and some of you took to the internet yourselves and broadcast activities such as story time directly into their homes.

Visits to the setting and settling in new families

For early years settings to continue they must always be ready to register new children and the 'usual' process would involve opportunities to come into the setting and visit. This provides a chance for the family and the child to explore the space, meet the staff and children and vice versa but allowing anyone into the setting not directly connected to the care giving was not possible, so here was another chance for the sector to adapt. Settings offered recorded videos of a "show-round" and some offered these live. Some settings sent personal messages to prospective families created by the key person, some created photo books and shared them, and some invited the families to join them for things like online story time. Every chance was taken to try and replicate the ways a family gets to see a new setting and for a child to feel welcomed. These strategies can also be used to support the settling in process once a family have registered and help a child feel safe being left with their key person.

Keeping in touch with families

Using online tools to communicate with families can mean it is easier to do this regularly and in smaller chunks of information. Sending three or four shorter messages across a day make it more likely the receiver will "hear" the message, if we put all four messages into one, some will be missed.

Safeguarding

Many practitioners have reported that more frequent contact through the use of technology has enabled them to build relationships with parents/carers who previously they may not have seen in the setting and this has led to stronger relationships and has strengthened their safeguarding practice as things are shared more openly.

Video calls have also enabled such meetings as "Team Around the Family" (TAFs) to happen and include more of the key people as they are easier for many to attend. It is of course worth remembering that having a video call can be a barrier to some people attending, especially parents so it is important to provide suitable alternatives for them such as making use of a private space in the setting to be able to attend.

Team meetings

It remains important that team members come together to discuss issues, share updates, and build relationships, if staff are not in the setting due to shielding, isolating, or for caring responsibilities it can be hard for them to come into the setting (even if they are on paid time). Technology can provide a solution by using video call technology to host the meeting. This might be used so that everyone can be at home and simply log in, but it can also be used in a blended way, where the core meeting happens in the setting but that others can call in via a video call and still fully participate in the meeting.

A note about a blended meeting though – it is a good idea to pair 1 remote attendee with someone in the room who takes responsibility to ensure their voice is heard throughout the meeting.

Reflective prompts – What next?

- How could a tech champion enhance your provision? What might the benefits be for your setting?

- What topic could you share with colleagues in a microlesson? How will you share it?

Challenge – create a microlesson for your colleagues on something you have learnt from reading this book and share it with others online by emailing it to me. I'll add it to my website for others to use. Don't be shy!

Conclusion

As you have just read, I feel very strongly that children can and should be a part of the tech strategy of any early years setting and I hope you will take the challenge to recruit a tech champion, or two to help you on this journey. I've given you some pointers about how to recruit them, whether an adult or a child, some person specifications, and a sample agreement to help set out what the expectations are. I hope they give you a strong starting point.

I've also covered microlearning as a tool to support your development and a way of sharing what you learn as you embark on the process embracing the tech.

As I was writing this book COVID hit the world and so it felt right to end the book with a section helping us to consider what the pandemic brought us in terms of technology enabling us to "carry on" and to notice what we have learnt and what we can continue to use as we create a new normal.

References and further reading

https://www.oxford-review.com/transfer-of-learning-into-the-workplace-does-classroom-learning-work/ 02/12/2019
https://learningpool.com/microlearning-macrolearning-benefits/ 02/12/2019
https://families.google/familylink/
https://en.wikipedia.org/wiki/Microlearning

Conclusion

Technology is here to stay and as I've already said will remain a part of our world for as long as the world exists. So, we have to educate ourselves, we have to play, and we have to find the technology that works for us. Like anything, it is a tool and with the right tool for the job, we do a better job. Finding the right tools to work with children, to support their learning and development is a key part of our role, and we can't stand still. As the world evolves so does the technology that forms a part of that. It becomes more complex, more exciting, more overwhelming. There is no rush, but we all need to commit to start somewhere. We all want the best for the children we work with, we all surely want the best for ourselves too. So I encourage you to embrace the learning journey, learn alongside your colleagues, your children, and their families and everyone will benefit. Make informed decisions, don't discount things through not knowing or through fear, ask questions, get curious, and keep playing.

DOI: 10.4324/9781003023173-10

Index

Note: **Bold** page numbers refer to tables